Pets and Farm Animals

Robin Kerrod

Facts On File

New York • Oxford

Distributed by
World Book, Inc.

PETS AND FARM ANIMALS
The Encyclopedia of the Animal World

Managing Editor: Lionel Bender
Art Editor: Ben White
Designer: Malcolm Smythe
Text Editor: Madeleine Samuel
Project Editor: Graham Bateman
Production: Clive Sparling, Joanna
    Turner

Media conversion and typesetting:
    Robert and Peter MacDonald,
    Una Macnamara

AN EQUINOX BOOK

Planned and produced by:
Equinox (Oxford) Limited,
Musterlin House, Jordan Hill Road,
Oxford OX2 8DP

Prepared by Lionheart Books

Library of Congress
Cataloging-in-Publication Data
Kerrod, Robin
    Pets and farm animals/Robin Kerrod
    p   cm.——(Encyclopedia of the Animal
    World)
    Bibliography: p.
    Includes index
    Summary: Introduces such domesticated
      animals as dogs, horses, mice,
      pigeons, goldfish, and bees.

1. Domestic animals – Juvenile literature.
[1. Domestic animals.] I. Title II. Series

SF75.5.K47 1989   636.088'7 - dc20
89-35001 CIP AC

ISBN 0-8160-1969-X

Published in North America by
Facts On File, Inc.,
460 Park Avenue South,
New York, N.Y. 10016

Origination by Alpha Reprographics Ltd,
Perivale, Middx, England

Printed in Hong Kong

10 9 8 7 6 5 4 3 2

FACT PANEL:
Key to symbols denoting general
features of animals

SYMBOLS NEXT TO HEADINGS

Diet

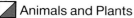 Other animals

■ Plants

◪ Animals and Plants

Breeding

◐ Seasonal (at fixed times)

◖ Non-seasonal (at any time)

CONTENTS

PREFACE

The National Wildlife Federation

For the wildlife of the world, 1936 was a very big year. That's when the National Wildlife Federation formed to help conserve the millions of species of animals and plants that call Earth their home. In trying to do such an important job, the Federation has grown to be the largest conservation group of its kind.

Today, plants and animals face more dangers than ever before. As the human population grows and takes over more and more land, the wild places of the world disappear. As people produce more and more chemicals and cars and other products to make life better for themselves, the environment often becomes worse for wildlife.

But there is some good news. Many animals are better off today than when the National Wildlife Federation began. Alligators, wild turkeys, deer, wood ducks, and others are thriving – thanks to the hard work of everyone who cares about wildlife.

The Federation's number one job has always been education. We teach kids the wonders of nature through *Your Big Backyard* and *Ranger Rick* magazines and our annual National Wildlife Week celebration. We teach grown-ups the importance of a clean environment through *National Wildlife* and *International Wildlife* magazines. And we help teachers teach about wildlife with our environmental education activity series called *Naturescope*.

The National Wildlife Federation is nearly five million people, all working as one. We all know that by helping wildlife, we are also helping ourselves. Together we have helped pass laws that have cleaned up our air and water, protected endangered species, and left grand old forests standing tall.

You can help too. Every time you plant a bush that becomes a home to a butterfly, every time you help clean a lake or river of trash, every time you walk instead of asking for a ride in a car – you are part of the wildlife team.

You are also doing your part by learning all you can about the wildlife of the world. That's why the National Wildlife Federation is happy to help bring you this Encyclopedia. We hope you enjoy it.

Jay D. Hair, President
National Wildlife Federation

INTRODUCTION

The *Encyclopedia of the Animal World* surveys the main groups and species of animals alive today. Written by a team of specialists, it includes the most current information and the newest ideas on animal behavior and survival. The Encyclopedia looks at how the shape and form of an animal reflect its life-style – the ways in which a creature's size, color, feeding methods and defenses have all evolved in relationship to a particular diet, climate and habitat. Discussed also are the ways in which human activities often disrupt natural ecosystems and threaten the survival of many species.

In this Encyclopedia the animals are grouped on the basis of their body structure and their evolution from common ancestors. Thus, there are single volumes or groups of volumes on mammals, birds, reptiles and amphibians, fish, insects and so on. Within these major categories, the animals are grouped according to their feeding habits or general life-styles. Because there is so much information on the animals in two of these major categories, there are four volumes devoted to mammals (*The Small Plant-Eaters; The Hunters; The Large Plant-Eaters; Primates, Insect-Eaters and Baleen Whales*) and three to birds (*The Waterbirds; The Aerial Hunters; The Plant- and Seed-Eaters*).

This volume, *Pets and Farm Animals*, includes entries on cats, dogs, horses, rats, mice, rabbits, budgerigars, pigeons, goldfish, cattle, sheep, goats, pigs, ducks, geese and bees. Together they number several hundred species and many thousands of breeds and varieties. Pet species are animals with which people have formed particularly close bonds around their homes. Farm animals are creatures that people keep for more practical purposes. (There are separate articles dealing with the general biology and life-styles of these animals in the appropriate volumes of this encyclopedia.)

People's relationship with pets such as cats, dogs and rabbits is mainly one of loving care and companionship. However, many dogs have been bred and trained primarily for guarding, hunting or herding. Horses have, over the centuries, been used in warfare, hunting, herding, sport and recreation. The domestic rat and mouse are bred mainly for the fascination of producing attractive varieties. The most rewarding feature of aquarium fish like goldfish and Siamese fighting fish is their beauty and ornamental qualities. Pigeons and ferrets are kept as pets for animal "beauty" competitions, sporting, recreational or working-partner purposes.

The commonest large mammals in the world are domestic cattle, sheep, pigs and goats. The development of civilization has depended on such farm animals and almost all societies depend on their use today. These creatures supply us with food (milk and meat) and with basic protection against the elements (furs, hides, wool for clothing). They are also used as working animals and beasts of burden. Other farm animals, such as ducks, geese and turkeys, are bred not only for food (meat and eggs), but also for ornamental reasons. Without these animals, our own survival would be in danger.

Each article in this Encyclopedia is devoted to an individual species or group of closely related species. The text starts with a short scene-setting story that highlights one or more of the animal's unique features. It then continues with details of the most interesting aspects of the animal's physical features and abilities, diet and feeding behavior, and general life-style. It also covers conservation and the animal's relationships with people.

A fact panel provides easy reference to the main features of distribution (natural, not introductions to other areas by humans), habitat, diet, size, color and breeding. (An explanation of the color-coded symbols is given on page 2 of the book.) The panel also includes a list of the common and scientific (Latin) names of species mentioned in the main text and photo captions. For species illustrated in major artwork panels but not described elsewhere, the names are given in the caption accompanying the artwork. In such illustrations, all animals are shown to scale; actual dimensions may be found in the text. To help the reader appreciate the size of the animals, in the upper right part of the page at the beginning of an article are scale drawings comparing the size of the species with that of a human being (or of a human foot).

Many species of animal are threatened with extinction as a result of human activities. In this Encyclopedia the following terms are used to show the status of a species as defined by the International Union for the Conservation of Nature and Natural Resources:

Endangered – in danger of extinction unless their habitat is no longer destroyed and they are not hunted by people.

Vulnerable – likely to become endangered in the near future.

Rare – exist in small numbers but neither endangered nor vulnerable at present.

A glossary provides definitions of technical terms used in the book. A common name and scientific (Latin) name index provide easy access to text and illustrations.

DOGS

A shepherd is driving a flock of sheep down from the hills to lower ground for the winter. From time to time little groups try to break away from the flock. But they don't get very far. Behind them, ever watchful, are two Collie sheepdogs. As soon as the dogs notice the breakaways, they dart quickly around them to head them off and force them back in line.

DOGS *Canis familiaris*

◼ Diet: meat, scraps; commercial dog foods: meat and cereal mixture.

◯ Breeding: up to 15 puppies in a litter, born after pregnancy of about 63 days.

Breeds: 1 species, up to 600 different breeds worldwide.

Distribution: worldwide with people; also feral (living not as pets but wild – strays) populations in many countries.

Size: smallest (Chihuahua): from 2lb; heaviest (St Bernard): up to 290lb; tallest (Irish Wolfhound): 40in at shoulders.

Color: highly variable; black, white, blue, brown, liver, cream, chestnut, gold; often standard color within breed, such as hounds: tricolor (black, white and tan), mottled (tricolor with black or tan spots on the white), pied (differently colored hairs mixed together).

Lifespan: up to 20 years, depending on breed.

People have used dogs to help them herd livestock since the time they first became farmers some 10,000 years ago. They have used dogs to help them hunt for even longer. Yet it is probable that dogs were first domesticated as pets, for which purpose they are kept mostly today.

POPULATIONS AND BREEDS

The United States is one of the top dog-owning countries, with a dog population of nearly 50 million. This works out at about 1 dog for every 5 people on average. In France there is about 1 dog for every 6 people, and in Britain, 1 for every 10.

Worldwide there are several hundred pure breeds of dog. But many dogs are not "purebred", they are cross-breeds, or mongrels. In many countries, there is a national organization that provides a register of breeds and lays down rules for breeding and showing dogs. They set the breed standards – those physical features deemed to be desirable in a breed.

▼ Basset Hounds are sturdy dogs with a good sense of smell, sometimes used in packs for hunting hares.

▲ A happy girl cuddles her pet puppy. She lives in the Amazon jungle in South America. Her mongrel puppy is only a few weeks old. When it has grown up, the men of her village will take it with them when they go hunting for game.

The first organization of this type was the Kennel Club in Britain, which was formed in 1873. The American Kennel Club was founded 11 years later, followed by similar organizations in other countries. Among the top breeds in the United States and Britain are the German Shepherd Dog, Golden Retrievers, Poodle, Yorkshire Terrier and Doberman Pinscher.

THE FIRST DOG

Scientists class all breeds of domestic dog under one species, *Canis familiaris*. From the genus name comes the adjective canine, meaning dog-like. It is now generally accepted that the dog descended from the Gray wolf (*Canis lupus*), and like the wolf, the dog is a carnivore – it eats meat.

The earliest known remains of a domestic dog, found in West Germany, date back to about 14,000 years ago. At this time Europe was emerging from the last Ice Age.

The practice of keeping dogs may have arisen in the following way: Stone Age hunters would sometimes have come across young wolf pups. They would have given some of the pups to their children to play with. The pups would have then grown up with the family as pets. When adult, the tame wolves would have started to breed. Their owners would probably have favored certain of the offspring for their looks or temperament, and driven away or killed the rest.

In this way Stone Age people most probably began a selective breeding process that eventually led to the many different breeds that exist today. As a result, most present-day breeds bear little resemblance to wolves.

SPORTING DOGS

Each country has a different method of classifying dog breeds, but two broad groups are generally recognized – sporting and non-sporting. The sporting dogs are those used for hunting, and include gundogs, hounds and terriers.

▲Dogs were common in ancient Egypt. This painting in the tomb of someone named Ipy, shows him with his pet dog. Ipy lived about 3,000 years ago.

▼These two sheepdogs are Kelpies, a type of Collie much used in Australia as working dogs.

▲**Breeds of non-sporting dog** Boston Terrier **(1)** (which originated in the USA in the 1800s), bred from the English Bulldog and a White English Terrier. Standard poodle **(2)** (France, 1500s), has a long coat that is often cut. Chow Chow **(3)** (China, BC), an ancient spitz breed.

►**Breeds of scent hound** Beagle (England, 1300s) **(4)**, once a favorite with royalty as a hunting dog. Bloodhound **(5)** (England, before 1100), noted for its ability to track game and people. Dachshund **(6)** (Germany, 1800s). American Foxhound **(7)** (USA, 1600s), less used in packs than the English Foxhound. Otterhound **(8)** (England, before 1200), has a waterproof coat.

▼**Breeds of sight hound** Irish Wolfhound **(9)** (Ireland 1100s), once used to hunt wolves, bears and stags. Whippet **(10)** (England, early 1900s), now widely used as a racing dog. Borzoi **(11)** (Russia, 1400s), an elegant dog that can run fast. Borzoi means swift in Russian.

1

2

3

4

5

6

7

8

9

10

11

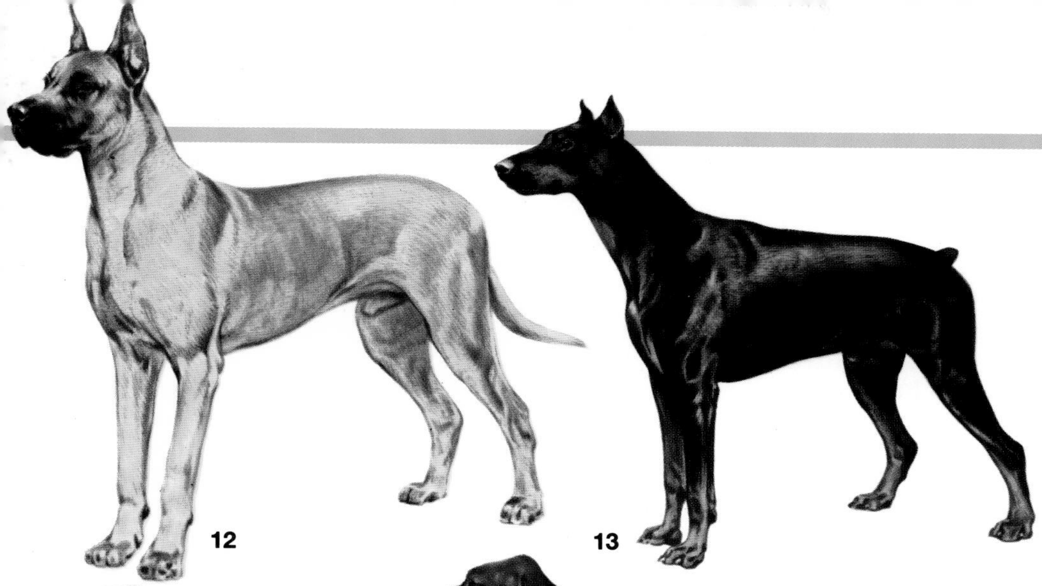

◀Breeds of guard dog Great Dane (12), indeed great in size, but not Danish; it is an ancient German breed. Doberman Pinscher (13) (Germany, 1865), a muscular, intelligent breed.

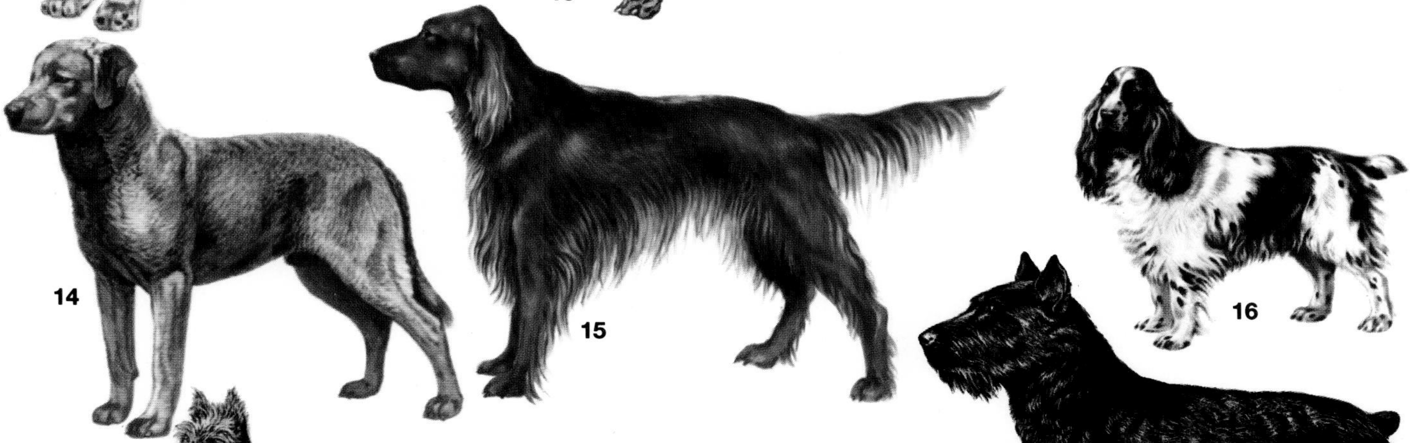

▼Breeds of gundog Chesapeake Bay Retriever (14) (USA, 1885), bred from dogs that survived a shipwreck. Irish Setter (15), also called Red Setter (Ireland, 1800s). Cocker Spaniel (16) (England, before 1300s).

◀Breeds of toy dog Chinese Crested Dog (17), an ancient Chinese breed. Chihuahua (18) (Mexico, before 1500s). Yorkshire Terrier (19) (England, 1800s).

▶Breeds of herding dog Bouvier des Flandres (20) (Belgium, early 1900s). Pembrokeshire Welsh Corgi (21) (Wales, 1100). Both were bred for guarding and herding cattle.

▼Breeds of terrier Cairn (22) (Scottish Highlands), Border (23) (border counties of Scotland), Skye (24) (Isle of Skye, Scotland) and Lakeland (25) (Lake District, England), all bred for centuries.

12

13

14

15

16

17

18

19

20

21

22

23

24

25

Gundogs are used mainly by sports-people hunting game birds such as pheasants and grouse. They need to be very obedient to work efficiently. One of their tasks is to show where the birds are hiding. Pointers do this by pointing – "freezing" in position with one foreleg raised and nose held high. The setters "set" in a half-sitting position when they scent a bird.

Retrievers are gundogs skilled at retrieving, or bringing back fallen birds. Spaniels can both find game and retrieve it, as can two continental European breeds, the Munsterlander and the Weimaraner.

Among the hounds, scent hounds are noted for their ability to follow the scent of animals, often over long distances. In some countries hunting with packs of hounds is a tradition, once considered useful in keeping down the numbers of vermin such as foxes, badgers and raccoons. But to-day such "blood sports" are widely condemned for being cruel.

Sight hounds are fleet-footed dogs that follow their quarry by sight. They can track much faster than they would if they relied on scent. Typical of this type of dog is the Greyhound.

Terriers are so called because of their ability to burrow in the earth (terre in French) to seek out their quarry. Most terrier breeds came originally from Britain. They were used to hunt rats, badgers and foxes.

NON-SPORTING DOGS

This group includes working dogs, which are breeds that have traditionally been used to help farmers herd cattle and sheep. It also contains breeds that are now purely used as pets, such as the Poodle, Dalmatian, Boston Terrier, Chow Chow and Bulldog. Many small dogs, known as toy dogs, too, such as the Chihuahua, Yorkshire Terrier, Pekinese and Pomeranian, are placed in this group.

Among the finest herding dogs are the Collies. They are swift, intelligent and obedient. Larger breeds, once used to protect the herds, are now trained as guard dogs. Outstanding among these are the Doberman Pinscher, Rottweiler and the German Shepherd Dog. They are widely used by the police and the military.

A working dog of a different kind is the huge St Bernard, a watchdog bred originally for the Bernadine Hospice in the Swiss Alps. It is best known for rescuing people lost in the mountains and victims of avalanches. Like the Bernese Mountain Dog, also from Switzerland, the St Bernard has sometimes been used as a draft animal (one used to pull heavy loads).

▼In East Africa, a hunter and his dog return from a successful hunt. Their hunter-gatherer way of life has changed little for thousands of years.

▶The Siberian Husky is traditionally used to pull sleds over snowy ground. It has a pointed muzzle and pointed ears.

CATS

A mother cat is padding along the garden path, past the rockery. One of her kittens hears her coming and hides behind a clump of flowers. As the cat draws near, the kitten tenses itself and gets ready to pounce. Its rear end shakes from side to side, and then it leaps at its mother, and the two tumble head over heels, clawing and kicking furiously. But it's only a play fight. This is the way the kitten learns how to hunt and fight.

After dogs, cats are the most popular domestic pets. There are nowhere near as many distinct breeds of cat as there are of dogs. Also, there are not so many differences in body form and behavior between the breeds as there are in dogs.

This has come about for two main reasons. First, cats have been domesticated for a shorter time, probably for less than 5,000 years. Second, cats have not been bred for working in the same way that dogs have. They have been, and still are, kept for their ability to catch rats and mice, but this is a natural instinct. Mostly, however, cats have been kept as companions.

SACRED AND PROFANE
The ancient Egyptians were probably the first to domesticate the cat. Cats would have been useful in keeping

down vermin attracted by the grain which the Egyptians stored. From about 1000 BC cats began to play an important role in Egyptian religion. Whole temples and priesthoods were devoted to looking after them. When cats died, they were often mummified in the same way as humans.

From Egypt, cats spread to other parts of the ancient world, and by the 4th century AD were very common throughout Europe. In the Middle

CATS *Felis sylvestris catus*

■ **Diet**: small mammals and birds; meat and fish, often with cereals, in commercial canned and dried foods.

◯ **Breeding**: 2-8 kittens, born after pregnancy of 60-69 days.

Breeds: 1 species, about 30 recognized breeds.

Distribution: worldwide with human population; feral (stray) cats also widespread.

Size: head and body length 20-24in; height at shoulders 10-11in; weight: queen (female) 5-10lb, tom (male) 6½-13lb.

Color: a range of tabby patterns is common, otherwise a wide range of colors and patterns: black, orange, brown, tortoise shell, white; many breeds have set color standards, for example, blue, lilac, chocolate.

Lifespan: on average about 12 years.

▲ Some of the body signals of cats. They often crouch in a defensive posture when threatened (1). Note the flattened ears. When threatened by, for example, a dog, they arch their back and spit (2). The hairs on the back and tail stand up, and the ears are again flattened. This is the friendly greeting posture (3), which cat owners know so well. The head and tail are held high and the ears are pricked.

◀ The face of pet cats is very similar to that of their wild relatives: the African wild cat (1) and the European wild cat (2), compared with the domestic cat (3).

Ages, cats were often persecuted and tortured in Europe because it was thought they had links with the Devil.

ANCESTORS

The cat the ancient Egyptians domesticated was the local African wild cat, *Felis sylvestris lybica*. It is thought that all domestic cats came originally from this breed. The African wild cat is a race of the Wild cat, *F. sylvestris*, found throughout Europe, Africa and Asia. From the genus name *Felis* comes the adjective feline, meaning cat-like.

In southern and eastern countries of the world, the domestic cat has tended to remain physically much like the ancient Egyptian cat, with a lean and lithe body. In northern Europe, however, cats have tended to become stockier (and larger) because of inter-breeding with the more heavily built European wild cat.

The Wild cat has a coat pattern that is commonly known as tabby. It has black stripes on an overall brownish-gray background. The background color, called agouti, is similar to that found in wild mice and rabbits. It provides excellent camouflage among vegetation.

COAT OF MANY COLORS

All the early domestic cats had a similar coat, and many still do today. As well as the striped or mackerel tabby coat, there is a blotched tabby, in which the stripes are broken.

Over the years there have been various mutations (changes) among domestic cats. This means that their genes (microscopic structures that determine an organism's characteristics) have altered slightly, and caused a change in the color of their coat. A change in the gene that produces the agouti background color has now resulted, for example, in the all-black cat. A blue coat occurs when black pigment is produced in "clumps," causing light and dark areas along the hairs. This makes the coat appear blue.

Another gene change causes all normally black pigments to become yellow or red, which results in the orange tabby. Orange tabbies are particularly common in South-east Asia and Japan.

▼A Blue Smoke Persian, with copper eyes. It has the typical round head and wide-set eyes of the Persian breed.

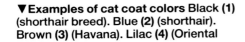

▼►Some breeds of cat This Siamese **(1)** is a Chocolate Point, with the typical brilliant blue eyes of the breed. The Manx Cat **(2)** is unmistakable because it has no tail. The tail of the Japanese Bobtail **(3)** is a mere stump. A Bicolored Persian **(4)** with copper eyes. Other bicoloreds have blue, red or cream with the white. The Angora **(5)**, or Turkish Angora, has the long silky coat of a Persian but a slimmer body. The Burmese **(6)** is a recent (1930s) breed. This one has a lilac coat. The Brown Tabby British Shorthair **(7)** has a short dense coat. The shaggy coated Maine Coone **(8)**. The Sphynx **(9)** is a near hairless cat first bred in Canada in 1966.

▼Examples of cat coat colors Black **(1)** (shorthair breed). Blue **(2)** (shorthair). Brown **(3)** (Havana). Lilac **(4)** (Oriental Shorthair). Seal point **(5)** (Siamese). Extreme Piebald **(6)** (Turkish Van). Shaded Silver **(7)** (Persian). Bicolored **(8)**, Orange tabby **(9)**, Tortoise shell **(10)** (all shorthair). Shell Cameo **(11)** (Persian). Smoke Cameo **(12)** (Persian).

4

5

6

7

8

9

◄Cats have a well-developed sense of balance. When they fall backwards out of a tree, for example, they twist their body around so that they hit the ground feet first. Their long legs act like shock absorbers to cushion their fall.

SHORTHAIRS AND LONGHAIRS

Nine out of every ten cats in the world are what are usually referred to as alley cats, or moggies. They have no pedigree, or pure breeding line. There are about 30 different breeds recognized by various countries.

Cat breeds can be grouped according to their length of coat and their body type. The British and American Shorthairs have a short, dense coat and a stocky appearance. They have been bred from selected short-haired domestic stock since the late 1800s.

Best known of the short haired cats with a slim body is the Siamese, one of the oriental breeds. It is thought to have come originally from Siam (now Thailand), and was introduced to the West in the 1890s. The pigmentation of its coat is limited to its face, ears, paws and tail.

The Persian, or Pedigree Longhair, is the best-known long-haired breed. It was bred in Europe in the 1800s by crossing cats imported from Persia (now Iran) and from Angora in Turkey. The Persian has a round broad head and a fine, long silky coat. The body is broad and the legs relatively short. Other longhairs include the slimmer Turkish Angora and the Himalayan. The Himalayan, also called the Colorpoint Longhair, is a crossbreed of the Persian and Siamese.

►An Abyssinian in mid-leap. The cat's long and strong hind legs make it a powerful jumper to overcome obstacles or to pounce on its prey.

►(inset) Few people can resist the appeal of fluffy kittens. They are cuddly, affectionate and full of fun.

DONKEYS

On a rocky hillside in Greece, the midday Sun beats down without mercy. A huge pile of straw is on the move, with a young boy walking alongside. Closer inspection reveals the head of a donkey poking out of the straw. It plods on despite its towering load, the rough ground and the heat. In such conditions donkeys provide the best means of transport.

The donkey has been a beast of burden for humans for thousands of years. Today, it is still widely used as a pack animal in many parts of the world. Donkeys are also ridden and used to pull carts and turn treadmills.

The donkey is extremely hardy and resistant to disease. It can exist on poor grazing and can tolerate heat and drought, which makes it particularly valuable in hot climates and desert regions. It also has a long working life and can be bred easily.

THE SMALLEST HORSE

The donkey is the smallest member of the horse family, and has the narrowest feet. It has a short erect mane, and its tail is brush-like with long hair just at the end. The most striking feature of the donkey, however, are its ears, which are large and long. They probably help to keep it cool by radiating away excess body heat.

The meat of the donkey is eaten in several countries. Its milk is high in protein and carbohydrates, but low

DONKEYS *Equus asinus* (or *E. africanus*)

■ **Diet:** mainly grass and hay; heavy, working donkeys benefit from grain.

○ **Breeding:** single foal born after pregnancy of 365-374 days.

Breeds: 1 species, more than 35 breeds.

Distribution: worldwide with humans, particularly in warm, arid climates in China, India, Africa and Central and South America. Found wild in the rocky deserts of Sudan, Ethiopia and Somalia; large feral populations in North and South America and Australia.

Size: height 9-15 hands (3-5ft); head and body length 6½-7¼ft; tail length 17-19in; average weight 570lb.

Color: gray, brown, black, white or piebald.

Lifespan: 40-50 years.

►**Breeds of donkey** The American Mammoth (1) is a heavily built donkey first bred in the USA in the 1700s by George Washington. The Muscat donkey (2) is a smaller animal from Arabia. The Sicilian, or Ragusan, ass (3) has small feet with hard hooves, and is excellent for mountain travel.

The donkey is also often called an ass, and the correct name of the male is jackass, or jack. The female is known as a jenny.

MULES AND HINNIES

Donkeys and horses can be made to interbreed, although they do not do so naturally in the wild. The offspring from a male donkey mating with a female horse is called a mule. The mating of a female donkey with a male horse produces an offspring known as a hinny. Both the mule and the hinny are infertile, which means that they cannot produce offspring.

The mule is more widely bred. It shares with the donkey a reputation for stubbornness, giving rise to the expression "as stubborn as a mule." It is bigger than the hinny and is thus more suitable as a beast of burden. Its head is shaped like that of a donkey, its tail more like that of a wild ass.

▼A Brazilian family rides home from market on their mule. Mules are tough animals with great stamina.

▲The donkey is a usually placid animal. It is found in hot arid climates, where horses could not survive.

in fats. For this reason it has long been used for feeding infants, the old and the sick. In ancient times bathing in asses' milk was considered to be good for the skin.

ASSES AND DONKEYS

The ancestor of the modern donkey was the African ass. This was first domesticated in North Africa about 6,000 years ago. A race of the African ass, called the Somali ass, still roams wild in Somalia and Ethiopia. It has a dark stripe on its back and stripes on its legs. The now extinct Nubian ass had a stripe on its shoulders, and this is now seen in some modern donkey breeds, such as the Sicilian, which have descended from it.

HORSES

Two great Shire Horses, their leather headgear studded with gleaming brass, stand harnessed to the plow. With a flick of the reins, the plowman sets them moving. He skillfully guides the steel plowshare into the ground to cut a straight furrow. The majestic Shires, weighing a ton apiece and standing almost 6ft tall at the withers, haul the plow with little apparent effort.

This scene, which evokes the countryside of the past, can still be seen at agricultural shows and plowing contests in the fall.

HORSES *Equus caballus*

 Diet: grass, hay, grains.

Breeding: single foal born after pregnancy of about 11 months.

Breeds: 1 species, about 200 breeds; Przewalski's horse is a separate species *E. przewalski*.

Distribution: worldwide with people; also large feral herds on most continents, such as the Mustangs in the western USA. Total world population about 65 million.

Size: smallest (Falabella): height under 7 hands (2⅓ft); largest (Shire): height over 18 hands (6ft).

Color: many shades: black, brown, chestnut, cream, gray and white: bays have a brown coat with black mane, tail and legs; roans have a coat flecked with white hairs; piebalds are black and white, skewbalds brown and white; palominos have a gold coat with silvery white mane and tail.

Lifespan: 25-35 years.

▼This Etruscan statue of an archer on horseback dates from about 800 BC. By this time horses had been bred large enough to be used as cavalry mounts. Earlier they had been used only to draw war chariots. In medieval times, they would carry heavily armored knights.

Horses have played an important part in the history of humankind. For almost 4,000 years, until the beginning of this century, they carried warriors into battle. Until the coming of the tractor, they were the major draft animals on many farms. Only with the development of the automobile did they cease to be the main means of transport. Today they are most widely ridden for pleasure and sport.

ANCIENT ANCESTORS
The remote ancestor of the horse was an animal called *Eohippus*, which stood only about 12in tall. It appeared in North America about 50 million years ago. After a long evolution, the last native horses of the New World were most likely hunted to extinction by people about 10,000 years ago, perhaps more recently. The horse from which all modern breeds are thought to have developed emerged at the end of the last Ice Age, 14,000 years ago.

A Polish soldier named Przewalski discovered descendants of this subspecies in Mongolia in 1881. It is often called Przewalski's Horse, or the Mongolian Wild Horse. It is now thought to be extinct in the wild, like its European cousin, the tarpan. Horses were reintroduced to the Americas by the Spanish in the 16th century AD. From these arose the wild horses of the plains, the Mustangs and the Criollos.

▲ Clearing a water jump at speed during a cross-country competition. In such events, horses and riders require courage and endurance to get over obstacles and gallop over difficult ground.

▼ **Horse breeds** The Falabella (1), now inbred. The pony-size Przewalski's Horse (2). The Heavy Draft Horse (3) developed from the medieval warhorse.

1

2

3

▲ Gypsy ponies grazing in a valley in Pakistan. The ancestors of today's gypsies were nomads from the Indian subcontinent.

▶ **Breeds of riding horse** The Appaloosa **(4)**, from the U.S. north-west, was originally bred by Indians from Mustangs. The American Quarter Horse **(5)** became the standard cow pony on cattle ranches. The Andalusian breed **(6)**, from Spain, dates back to the 700s. The Pinto **(7)** was bred by the Plains Indians of North America. The Hanoverian **(8)**, from Germany, is a particularly popular show jumping horse. The Thoroughbred **(9)**, which originated in England, is the fleetest of horses.

◀▼ **Breeds of draft horse** The Italian Heavy Draft **(1)** of north and central Italy. The Belgian or Brabant **(2)**. The Percheron **(3)**, the most popular cart-horse in the world.

1

2

3

PONY BREEDS

The tarpan stands about 4½ft tall at the withers, or the high point between the back and the neck. The height of a horse is usually expressed in hands, one hand being 4in. So the tarpan is 13 hands high.

By convention, an animal of 14.2 hands or less is classed as a pony. Larger animals are classed as horses.

There are more than 30 recognized breeds of ponies. In general, they are hardy, intelligent and independent animals. They have not been changed by humans as much as horse breeds have. They have all tended to evolve gradually by the process of natural selection.

The Fjord and the Viatka (Russia) ponies are interesting in having a stripe along the back and zebra markings on the forelegs like the tarpan. Most ponies have a long mane and forelock, and grow a thick coat to ward off the winter cold. The Shetland grows a particularly thick, shaggy coat. With a height of some 9 hands, it is the smallest natural horse breed.

HOT BLOOD AND COLD BLOOD

The selective breeding of horses began soon after the animals had been domesticated about 5,000 years ago. Larger animals were bred so that they could carry soldiers into battle. Later the Romans began to develop even

larger breeds, which evolved into the great warhorses of the Middle Ages. The heavy draft horses, such as the Shire and Belgian breeds, are their modern descendants. These animals, standing some 17 or 18 hands high, are docile and good natured. They are often termed cold-blooded.

The build, temperament and gait of all the heavy draft horses contrasts greatly with those of ancient breeds from the Middle East and North Africa. These breeds include the Turkoman from Persia (now Iran), and the Arabian from the Arabian Peninsula. They are intelligent, swift and spirited animals and for this reason they are termed hot-blooded.

23

Historically, the most important crossbreeding took place in England in the late 1600s and early 1700s. Three Arab males (stallions), the Byerly Turk, the Darley Arabian and the Godolphin Arabian, were mated with English racing females (mares) to produce what are considered to be the finest horses of all, the Thoroughbreds. These are the fastest of all horses – up to 40mph – and are bred as racehorses. They are also crossed with other breeds.

In the United States, Quarter Horses are often raced. Racing types have been bred by crossing cow ponies, a cattle-herding breed, with Thoroughbreds. This type of horse is so called because it was originally raced over a quarter-mile (440yd) course.

RIDING AND HARNESS HORSES

The majority of the horse breeds used for riding are often termed warm-blooded, because they have a certain amount of the "hot blood" of the Arabian in their make-up. Many hunters, for example, are a cross between a Thoroughbred and a heavy horse such as the Cleveland Bay and the Irish Draft. Hunters are used, for example, in fox hunting and in cross-country events such as cross-country races. They need to be swift and to have great stamina.

An ordinary riding horse is often called a hack. Many are bred from native pony breeds. Cobs are often used for pleasure riding and sometimes for hunting. They are strong, sturdy animals, which are not particularly fast, but have great stamina. Typical is the Welsh Cob, bred from the Welsh Mountain Pony. It is often crossed with Thoroughbreds to make good hunters.

The most distinctive of the harness breeds is the Hackney. Hackneys have a characteristic high-stepping gait. They were originally bred in England by crossing Norfolk Trotters with Arabians and Thoroughbreds. There is Hackney blood in the American Standardbred, a popular breed for harness racing.

▼An Arabian colt (young male horse), only a few weeks old. It will grow into one of the most graceful of all horses.

▶Tribesmen brandishing weapons at a Berber festival in Morocco. Traditionally they ride Arabians and Barbs.

FERRETS

Nets have been set over all but one of the holes in the rabbit warren. The ferreter puts his albino ferret by the open hole, and down it goes. After about 10 minutes a startled rabbit bolts into one of the nets. But it is not set properly, and the rabbit wriggles free and escapes. The ferret emerges seconds later. It doesn't try to follow the rabbit because it is well-trained, and trots back to its master.

Ferreting has been a traditional means of controlling vermin for centuries. Ferrets were kept for that purpose in ancient Greece and Rome. They were probably used then mainly for keeping down mice and rats. Later, they were used for controlling rabbits. Nowadays, methods such as gassing and poisoning are used for large scale extermination of rodents and rabbits.

Ferreting for rabbits and rats is still practised in many European countries as a sport. In other countries, including the United States, ferrets are kept mainly as pets. Indeed, in most US states it is illegal to use ferrets for any form of hunting at all. In a few countries, ferrets are farmed for their fur, called fitch.

▼ An American mink, pictured in a quarry in Scotland. This relative of the ferret has escaped from a nearby mink farm and gone wild, becoming a pest to poultry.

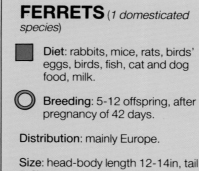

FERRETS (*1 domesticated species*)

■ Diet: rabbits, mice, rats, birds' eggs, birds, fish, cat and dog food, milk.

○ Breeding: 5-12 offspring, after pregnancy of 42 days.

Distribution: mainly Europe.

Size: head-body length 12-14in, tail 5-6in.

Color: polecat ferret: brownish-black coat; albino: yellowish-white.

Lifespan: 6-8 years.

Species mentioned in text:
Black-footed ferret (*Mustela nigripes*)
European polecat (*M. putorius putorius*)
Ferret (*M. p. furo*)
Steppe polecat (*M. eversmanni*)

TAME POLECATS
The ferret is a member of the weasel family, Mustelidae. It is the domesticated form of a wild polecat. It may have descended from the European polecat or the Steppe polecat of Russia and China. It is not closely related to the Black-footed ferret of the western United States.

The scientific name of the ferret is *Mustella putorius furo*, meaning "smelly weasel thief." This refers to the ferret's unpleasant smell, which comes from an oily liquid given off from glands at the tail. It produces a little of this in its feces to mark its territory. It produces a lot when frightened or angry.

Like all the other members of the family, ferrets are carnivores, or meat-eaters. They will kill mice, rats, fowl and rabbits, which are much larger than they are. The female ferret is called a jill or doe; the male, a hob or dog; and the offspring, kits or kittens.

TWO VARIETIES
There are two varieties of ferret, the polecat and the albino. The polecat is the colored form, normally with a similar coat to the wild polecat. It has black eyes and its hair is brownish-black at the tips, but pale underneath. There are yellowish markings on the face and along the top of the ears. A sandy coat form has also become popular.

The albino ferret is all-white, with pink eyes. The "whiteness" may vary greatly from cream to orange-yellow.

FERRETS AT WORK
Most ferreters use the smaller jills to go hunting. They are used as "loose" ferrets – set loose down warren holes to flush out rabbits. Sometimes when

◄A ferreter with an albino line ferret and a spade. He sends the ferret down a rabbit-hole to drive out a loose ferret that has made a kill underground. The line ferret takes over the kill, and the ferreter then has to dig it out.

▼A nursing jill and her litter of kits. They were born 9 days ago, when they were only about 1in long and weighed about ¾ ounce. They will not open their eyes for at least another 2 weeks.

a jill corners a rabbit underground, it kills and eats it. So it has to be flushed out, usually by a so-called line ferret, which is one wearing a collar with a line attached. The line ferret will chase off the jill, which will return to the surface. Then it will start to feed itself. And the ferreter has to dig it out.

FERRETS AS PETS

Ferrets are lively, inquisitive and intelligent creatures that can be quite easily trained. They can be handled by children. Despite their strong smell, ferrets are extremely clean creatures, forever grooming themselves.

Ferrets should be kept outside in a spot sheltered from the sun, wind and rain. They can be kept in cages, or cubs, like rabbit hutches, which have a small run as well as enclosed sleeping quarters. Or they can be kept in small buildings called courts, which are rather like a garden aviary.

RATS

It is the favorite time of day for the all-black, black-eyed rat. Its mistress has come home from school and opened the cage door. Off the table, on to the bedspread, down to the floor it races. Then it leaps on to the bookshelf and up on to the window sill. There it sits for a while, before jumping on to its mistress's shoulder.

In the wild, rats are among mankind's worst pests, damaging crops, gnawing through wooden buildings and carrying disease. The worst offenders are the Brown rat (also called the Common or Norway rat) and the Black rat (or Roof rat, *Rattus rattus*).

▼A Hooded male rat grooms a Cream female. Hooded varieties have a mainly white body, with colored head, throat and shoulders and band along the spine to the naked tail.

▲In a large cage filled with garden material for nesting, these 4-day pet rats huddle together for warmth and comfort.

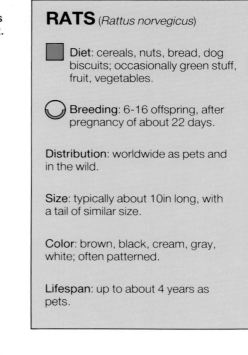

RATS (*Rattus norvegicus*)

■ Diet: cereals, nuts, bread, dog biscuits; occasionally green stuff, fruit, vegetables.

◯ Breeding: 6-16 offspring, after pregnancy of about 22 days.

Distribution: worldwide as pets and in the wild.

Size: typically about 10in long, with a tail of similar size.

Color: brown, black, cream, gray, white; often patterned.

Lifespan: up to about 4 years as pets.

IN SEWERS AND IN HOMES

Both the Brown rat and the Black rat are found in huge numbers in association with people. The Brown rat is the more widespread in temperate regions and is the type commonly found in city sewers. Black rats are found mostly in tropical regions. Both species originated in Asia and spread with the growth of commerce.

All domesticated rats are derived from the Brown rat. They make excellent pets when well looked after and handled properly. Large numbers are bred for use in medical research and in experiments on animal behavior.

▼A pet White rat, an albino variety of the Brown rat. It is white all over and has pink eyes.

INTELLIGENT AND CLEAN

Rats are not kept as pets in such large numbers as mice. Nor are they available in such a range of varieties. This is because they have been domesticated for a much shorter period, namely a little over a century. However, rats are more intelligent than mice, they are docile, and they keep themselves exceptionally clean. They do not have the unpleasant smell typical of mice.

Because rats are so big, they require a large cage. They also need a variety of playthings, such as cotton reels, little plastic shapes and tubing. Small tree branches or wooden blocks will allow them to climb and let them gnaw. Like all rodents, rats need to gnaw to keep their continuously growing incisor teeth in good condition.

COLORS AND PATTERNS

Rats have been bred in a number of color varieties and coat patterns. The Agouti has much the same coloring as the wild rat. It is a rich brown, with gray underneath. The outer, guard hairs are black, as are the eyes. The belly is silver. The Cinnamon Pearl has color bands of cream, blue and orange, and silver guard hairs and belly. The Siamese has a beige body that darkens towards the tail.

There are a number of recognized patterns for coats. A familiar type is the Berkshire, which is any main color with a white chest and belly, white patches on the limbs and tail, and a white spot on the forehead. Only one type of coat is known, the rex, which is a rough coat.

MICE

A Chocolate Dutch doe mouse has given birth to 12 cubs, but she doesn't have enough milk for them all. Fortunately, the breeder has a Himalayan doe that has lost most of her cubs and has plenty of milk. So he rolls six of the Dutch cubs in the urine of the Himalayan doe and places them in her nest. The smell of the urine masks the cubs' "strange" smell and allows the foster doe to accept them as her own.

All domesticated mice are derived from the wild House mouse, a species that came originally from central Asia. Wild mice began living with people about 10,000 years ago. That is when humans first developed farming and began to store grain in large quantities on which the mice could feed.

Mice were first domesticated in the Far East several centuries ago. By the 1700s, several fancy breeds had become established in Japan, including chocolate-colored, albino (white) and black mice. There were also so-called Waltzing Mice, which "danced" because of a defect in their balance organs. Since then many more varieties with different colored coats have been selectively bred.

JUST LIKE ANY OTHER MOUSE
As well as fancy breeds for showing and keeping as pets, large numbers of mice are bred as laboratory animals. By continuous inbreeding, a "standard mouse" has been bred among which all individuals carry the same genes and are virtually identical to one another. This makes it easier for scientists to compare the effects on different mice of different treatments.

▶ Two Albino Mice. Several mice can be kept in the same cage, but only if they are reared together. (All males eventually fight savagely, even littermates.)

MICE (*Mus musculus*)

■ Diet: cereals, nuts, bread, dog biscuits; occasionally fruit and vegetables.

◯ Breeding: 8-12 offspring, after pregnancy of about 21 days.

Distribution: worldwide in the wild and as pets.

Size: about 3in long, with a tail of similar size.

Color: brown, chocolate, cream, silver, gold, black, white; often patterned.

Lifespan: up to about 2 years as pets.

Tame mice differ from wild ones in that they are docile and easy to handle; they have a larger body and a longer tail; and their ears are bigger and their eyes more prominent.

SELFS AND SATINS
The so-called self-colored varieties of mouse, or selfs, are the same color all over. They include black, blue, chocolate, red and cream. These have black eyes. Champagne, fawn, silver and white varieties have pink eyes. Tans are varieties that have one of the recognized colors for the main coat, but with a golden-tan belly.

Some of the most distinctive mice have a marked, or patterned coat. The Dutch has similar markings to the Dutch rabbit – a white nose, colored

▲A nest of laboratory mice, with young of various colors.

cheeks, white forepart of the body, but a colored hindpart. The beige-coated Siamese has similar markings ("points") to the Siamese Cat, with brown-tipped hairs on the nose, ears, feet and tail.

Various types of coat are found in domestic mice. In the rex the coat is tightly curled, and in the astrex it is loosely waved. Longhairs have a silky coat nearly twice the normal length. Satins have a coat with a sheen to it.

QUICK-BREEDERS

Mice breed as readily in captivity as they do in the wild. The females start to come on heat at the age of about 6 to 7 weeks, and every 4 or 5 days thereafter. The buck (male) mouse should be allowed in with the doe (female) for a while to allow mating to take place, but then removed. The doe gives birth 3 weeks later to about 10 young, called cubs. They are born blind, deaf and naked. Their eyes do not open until about a week later.

At this stage, the buck should not be allowed back with the doe because she can become pregnant again immediately after she has given birth. If breeding were allowed to continue freely, the doe could produce as many as 100 cubs in a year!

▲▼Color difference among varieties of mice (The mice shown are all females.) Chocolate Belted Mouse (1) drinking from a water bottle. Chocolate has been a favorite coat color for centuries. Himalayan Mouse (2) feeding on grain. This variety has red eyes, but some have black eyes. Lilac Mouse (3). Black and Tan Mouse (4) sniffing the ground. Yellow Mouse (5) eating.

HAMSTERS AND GERBILS

It is mid-evening and a pet hamster has just woken up after spending most of the day asleep. It crawls out of its nesting box and sees in the feeding bowl its favorite food – sunflower seeds. Sitting on its hind legs, it holds the seeds with its front paws and splits them open with its sharp teeth. It swallows a few, but stuffs most of them into its cheek pouches. It doesn't stop eating until its cheek pouches are bulging.

▼ Gerbils make delightful pets and quickly get used to being handled. They should never be picked up by the tail.

HAMSTERS AND GERBILS (2 main species)

■ Diet: grains, carrots, fruit.

◯ Breeding: hamsters: 2-8 offspring, after pregnancy of 16 days; gerbils: 3-5 offspring, after pregnancy of 25 days.

Distribution: worldwide as pets.

Size: hamster: length about 6in; gerbil: length about 4in.

Color: hamster: mainly golden, cream, or gray; gerbil: commonly sandy brown with dark stripe along back and black-tipped tail.

Lifespan: hamsters 18-24 months; gerbils 3-5 years.

Hamsters almost always stuff food into their cheek pouches when they eat. Afterwards they empty out the food in another part of the cage or in their nesting box. They may keep a number of food stores, and return to them when they get hungry. The name hamster is very appropriate because it comes from the German word meaning hoard.

ALL FROM ONE MOTHER

All pet hamsters belong to the same species, the Golden hamster (*Mesocricetus auratus*). They are descended from just one female and her litter of 12 young, which were collected near Aleppo, Syria, in 1930. The standard color is chestnut brown, often with dark markings on the shoulders. The belly is creamy white. Other colors have also been bred.

Hamsters are in the main solitary creatures and must usually be kept apart, except when breeding. Breeding is something they do very readily. They become sexually mature after about 2 months. They give birth just over 3 weeks after mating, and can become pregnant again a month later.

SAND RATS

Gerbils are also prolific breeders. Females can become pregnant again a few days after giving birth. They could have up to 10 litters in a year!

Unlike hamsters, gerbils are very sociable creatures that like to live in a group. They also squat on their hind legs and eat food with their forepaws. Again, sunflower seeds are a favorite.

The gerbils commonly kept as pets are Mongolian gerbils (*Meriones unguiculatus*), often called Sand rats. They are very clean to keep and do not smell. This is because their feces are hard and dry and they produce only a few drops of urine a day.

▶ A Satin bronze hamster female, with her cheek pouches full. Satin varieties have a glossy rich-colored coat.

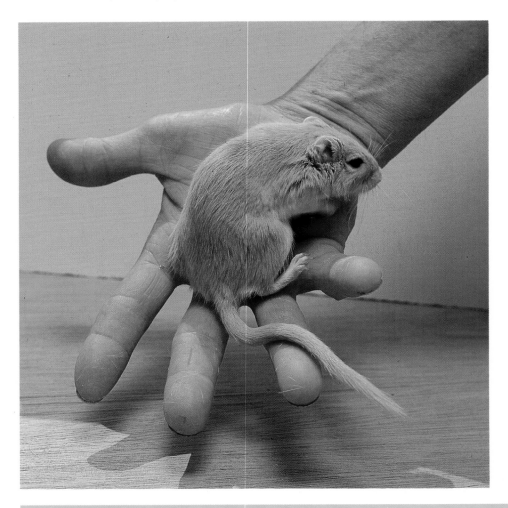

CAVIES OR GUINEA PIGS

The occupants of the hutches in the backyard have been quiet all day, except for the occasional whistle and squeak. But now, as they hear someone approaching (perhaps with food), they begin to squeal, just like pigs do when they're excited. This has earned the animals, properly called cavies, the name of Guinea pigs.

►In many South American villages people still breed cavies for meat. The flesh of the animal tastes similar to pork. This might have been another reason for calling the animal a "pig."

CAVIES OR GUINEA PIGS (*4 main related species*)

■ Diet: grass and other greenstuff; coypus: water plants, mussels, snails.

◐ Breeding: Pet cavy: 2-4 offspring, after pregnancy of about 67 days; chinchilla: 1-4 offspring; coypu: 5-7 offspring; both after pregnancy of 4 months.

Distribution: worldwide.

Size: head-body length: Pet cavy 10-12in, no tail; chinchilla about 10in, tail 3in; coypu: up to 24in, tail 16in.

Color: Pet cavy: white, cream, black, brown, red; often patterned; chinchilla: usually silver gray; coypu: reddish-brown.

Lifespan: Guinea pig 8 years as pet; coypu 6 years; chinchilla 20 years.

Species mentioned in text:
Brazilian cavy (*Cavia aperea*)
Chinchilla (*Chinchilla lanigera*)
Coypu (*Myocastor coypus*)
Pet cavy (*Cavia porcellus*)

The Pet cavy is one of 14 species in the cavy family, Caviidae. Cavies are rodents, and they are all native to South America. The "pet" species was first domesticated there by the Incas, maybe as long as 1,000 years ago. The Spaniards introduced the animals to Europe in the late 1500s. They have since gradually become popular pets the world over.

The name Guinea may have come about for two reasons. First, ships traveling from South America towards Europe usually visited the Guinea coast of West Africa. Second, "Guinea" became accepted as the spelling for the South American region of Guiana, from where the animals were first shipped.

PETS AND PATIENTS

Like its wild relatives, the Pet cavy has a short, rotund body with an exceptionally large head. Its eyes, too, are large. Its closest relative in the wild is the Brazilian cavy, a creature of the grasslands. Like most other wild cavies, this has the typical agouti, brownish-gray coat.

Domesticated cavies, however, are found in a wide variety of colors. This is as a result of several centuries of selective breeding by humans. Cavies

►A Pet cavy sow and its pups. The young pups can take solid food and survive on their own if they have to after only a week or so.

▼The chinchilla is a cavy-like rodent that is a native of the high Andes in South America. It grows a thick, soft coat which keeps it warm in the cold conditions. Some chinchillas are kept as pets.

are not only bred to be pets. They are also bred for use in experiments in biological and medical research laboratories. (Some people argue that such experiments cause unnecessary pain and should be stopped.)

COLORS AND COATS
As with mice and rats, Pet cavies that have the same color coat all over are called self-coloreds, or selfs. The colors include white, chocolate, red, black, cream and lilac. Among the patterned varieties, one of the most attractive is the Tortoise shell. A variety with a white body and colored points (body extremeties) is also very popular. It is called the Himalayan.

Pet cavies may also have different types of coat, in any of the colors. Peruvians have a coat that is long and silky. Abyssinians have a coat with rosettes and ruffs of hair.

RAISED ON FARMS
In South America, there are many other species of rodents that broadly resemble the cavies. They represent 11 different families. Some, such as the pacarana, agouti and viscacha, are hunted for their meat or fur, but have not been domesticated. Two species have, however, and both are now bred widely for their fur. One is the coypu, a water creature, which has webbed hind feet for swimming. It

has a long, coarse outer coat, but a very soft underfur. It is raised on farms for its fur, which is known as nutria.

In several countries, coypus have escaped from fur farms and returned to the wild. Large feral populations have become established, and they cause a great deal of damage by ravaging crops and burrowing into river banks.

The other South American rodent raised on farms for its fur is the chinchilla. Its coat is believed to be denser than that of any other mammal. The usual coat color is silvery gray, but dark-colored varieties, such as the Charcoal and a White, have been bred by fanciers.

RABBITS

It is 25 days since the buck and the doe mated. Now the doe starts to make a nest. She carries hay into the nestbox and fussily arranges it. Then she plucks fur from her belly to line the nest. This is a sure sign that her pregnancy is coming to an end. Thirty days after mating, in the privacy of her nest, the doe gives birth.

All domesticated rabbits, kept as pets or raised for their meat or fur, are descended from a single species, the European rabbit. Originally this lived only in the Iberian peninsula (modern Spain and Portugal) and southern France. About 2,000 years ago the Romans began to take rabbits to Italy and raise them for meat. Over the years many of the rabbits escaped and started to breed in the wild. By the Middle Ages, they were common throughout Europe.

RABBITS (Oryctolagus cuniculus)

■ **Diet:** grass and other vegetation; bark in winter; cereals and soya beans often used as supplementary feed on rabbit farms.

◔ **Breeding:** litter of 3-10 young after pregnancy of 30-34 days.

Breeds: about 150 recognized breeds and varieties.

Distribution: kept as pets and raised for meat worldwide. Introduced rabbits gone wild in many countries; they often, as in Australia, reach pest proportions and ravage crops.

Size: length 12-24in, weight 11-26lb.

Color: black, white, browns, grays.

Lifespan: up to 12 years as pets.

Rabbits were first tamed by monks in monasteries, where the first selective breeding took place. Since then a fascinating variety of breeds, with coats of different colors and different hair types, have become available.

BRED FOR MEAT OR FUR

Rabbits are bred for meat mainly in Asia and Africa, where Ghana alone produces more than 5 million carcasses a year. In Europe, Italy is the main rabbit-meat producer. The two major meat breeds are the New Zealand White and the Californian. They weigh up to 11lb when fully grown, but they are usually marketed when they are about 8 weeks old and weigh about 4lb. On some rabbit farms the Flemish Giant is raised. This, the largest domestic rabbit, weighs up to 22lb when fully grown.

The most important fur breeds are the Chinchilla and the Angora. The Chinchilla is sometimes bred for its pelt (skin with fur), which is similar to that of the wild chinchilla, a cavy-like rodent. The Angora is a long-haired breed, whose coat can be clipped to provide wool.

COATS OF MANY COLORS

The shiny coated Dutch breed is one of the oldest fancy breeds and one of the most popular. The English is also a popular old breed. It is mainly white, with colored nose and ears and spots on its coat. The Himalayan is another attractive rabbit. It is mainly white, with nose, eyes, ears, feet and tail colored blue, chocolate or lilac.

The most strikingly colored rabbit is the Harlequin. The coat of this long-haired breed carries a pattern of orange and black stripes. It is sometimes called the "Football Jersey Rabbit". The Magpie has a similar pattern, but in black and white. Some rabbits have a particularly short, dense coat that looks like velvet. They are known as Rex. Those with a tight, wavy coat are called Astrex.

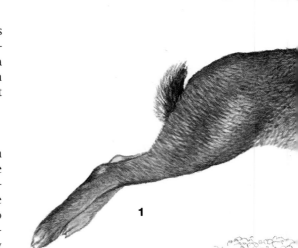

► **Breeds and varieties of rabbit** A buck (male) Belgian Hare (1) chases a Silver Fox (2) doe (female) during a courtship routine. A male Chinchilla Gigantea (3) rubs its scent on a twig to mark its territory. It is valued for its fur. A female Brown and Gray Lop (4) grooms itself. The Lop is an ancient breed noted for its exceptionally long ears. These have resulted from many years of selective breeding. This attractive rabbit is a Californian male (5). It is standing upright in a scanning posture.

▼ A Chocolate Dutch doe and young. This is one of the most attractive of the fancy breeds of rabbit.

CANARIES AND FINCHES

A cage is by the open window, and the yellow bird inside is "singing its heart out." Pure, clear, melodious notes and exhilarating trills pour forth from its throat. Only one bird is capable of such a virtuoso performance – the canary.

The canary has been kept for its singing ability for over 400 years. The bird is a native of the Canary Islands off North Africa, and is also found on the islands of the Madeira and Azores groups. The wild canary has a mainly greenish-gray plumage, with yellowish underparts.

BRIGHT COLORS
Several domesticated canaries, called Greens, are bred with the wild color and markings. Most canaries, though, have mainly yellow plumage, with white or dark flight feathers and tail. An all-red variety has also become popular among canary fanciers. It was produced as a result of cross-breeding between canaries and a finch called the Red siskin from South America.

Cross-breeding between the other finches and canaries produces offspring that are known as mules. The Red siskin mule is fertile, but most mules are sterile and cannot themselves be bred from. Attractive mules come from cross-breeding the canary with the goldfinch and greenfinch.

Some of the best singing canaries were bred originally in the Hartz Mountains of Germany. Known as Rollers, they trill almost continuously as they sing. Only the males sing.

OTHER EXOTIC BIRDS
Bengalese finches are popular cage birds because they are tame, hardy and easy to breed in captivity. In the Far East, they have been kept as pets for at least 250 years. Only the males sing, making a kind of humming or rattling sound.

The breeding instincts of finches are strong, and they are often used by bird fanciers to foster other species. Those of a single color are popularly

▼A trio of Java sparrows. The White variety, seen here between two Pieds, is a particularly good breeder.

CANARIES AND FINCHES *(about 30 species)*

■ Diet: seeds, fresh green stuff.

○ Breeding: canary: 3-5 eggs, 13 or 14 days incubation; Bengalese finch: 5-6 eggs, 15-19 days incubation.

Breeds: 250+ breeds and varieties.

Distribution: worldwide as pets; canaries particularly in Europe and the US; finches mainly in Japan.

Size: canary: length 4-8in; Bengalese finch: length 4in.

Color: canary: usually yellow, with white or black; also reds, blues, greens and grays; Bengalese finch: chestnut, fawn, usually with white.

Lifespan: canary: 10-15 years; Bengalese finch up to 4 years.

Species mentioned in text:
Bengalese finch (*Lonchura striata*)
Canary (*Serinus canaria*)
Goldfinch (*Carduelis carduelis*)
Greenfinch (*C. chloris*)
Java sparrow (*Padda oryzivora*)
Zebra finch (*Peophila guttata*)

▲Color variation in canary breeds
London (1). Lizard (clear-capped gold)
(2). Fife (clear yellow) (3). Border (buff)
(4). Red orange (5). Roller (6), singing.

▶These Rose Pastel canaries have a
heavy body, like that of the Border
breed. The red pigment was introduced
into canary breeds in the 1920s.

known as selfs. The Chocolate Selfs
look most like the wild ancestor of the
Bengalese finch.

Two other species of small finch
related to the Bengalese finch are also
popular. They are the Zebra finch and
the Java sparrow. The Zebra finch,
found wild in Australia, can be bred
easily. The most popular variety has
the plumage of the wild bird, mainly
gray, with chestnut patches on the
cheeks and flanks in the males.

The Java sparrow was first domesticated in the Far East some two
centuries ago. It is noted for its
endearing habit of sleeping under or
next to certain species of dove.

BUDGERIGARS

The unmistakable sounds and smells of breakfast are coming from the kitchen as mother lays the table.

"Good morning." "Good morning Mom." "Hurry up you're late." "Tea or coffee?"

It seems that all the family are down for breakfast. But they aren't. Apart from mother, there is no other person about. It is an African gray parrot that is doing the talking. It is repeating words it hears at breakfast time almost every day.

BUDGERIGARS (*about 150 domesticated species*)

Diet: seeds, green foods such as lettuce, cabbage, carrot tops, fruit.

Breeding: 4-8 eggs; incubation period: 17-19 days budgerigars, up to 35 days for some parrots.

Breeds: several hundred varieties.

Distribution: worldwide as pets.

Size: budgerigars: length 7-8in; other parrots: length 4-40in.

Color: green, yellow, gray, blue, white, mauve; budgerigars usually have black bars on back of head.

Lifespan: budgerigars: 8 years or more; some parrots: 30-50 years.

Species mentioned in text:
African gray parrot (*Psittacus erithacus*)
Amazon parrots (*Amazona* species)
Budgerigar (*Melopsittacus undulatus*)
Canary-winged bee bee (*Brotogeris versicolorus chiriri*)
Cockatiel (*Nymphicus hollandicus*)
Lovebirds (*Agapornis* species)
Macaws (*Ara* species)
Sun conure (*Aratinga solstitialis*)

▲During courtship, cock budgerigars may often be seen feeding the hens. Here a Skyblue cock feeds an Albino hen on regurgitated seed.

◄In a bird market in Jakarta, Indonesia, budgies, parrots and other domesticated birds for sale are on display.

▼A cock cockatiel, with its crest erect. It is a smaller version of the cockatoo, another popular cage bird. Both came originally from Australia.

Budgerigars and parrots are the most popular of all cage birds. They are colorful and affectionate, and can be taught to talk. But they can also be dirty, noisy and demand a great deal of attention. They all belong to the parrot family, Psittacidae.

In the wild, budgerigars live in the interior of Australia, where they are often found in flocks of hundreds of thousands. The Aborigines call the bird "betcherrygah," which means good food. Other names for it include Shell parrot, Grass parakeet, and often just parakeet. Most budgerigars, or budgies, found in pet shops are now bred in captivity, and this is the only way such birds should be obtained. Collecting specimens from the wild has serious effects on natural populations. International trade in wild parrots and similar cage birds is now effectively banned, but it still goes on illegally on a large scale. The pet birds are larger than the wild ones.

NOT SO QUICK TO LEARN
Among wild budgerigars, only the cocks (males) sing, though both sexes make calls. The birds do not mimic the calls of other species. Cage birds are different. The cocks in particular mimic the human voice and "talk." The birds must be trained as soon as they can fend for themselves, a few days after being able to fly. They must also be kept apart from other birds, or they will just chatter with them and not talk to humans.

To train the bird, hold it close to your lips and repeat the word you want it to learn, over and over again. Some budgies pick up their first word in less than a month, although others take much longer.

GLORIOUS COLORS
Wild budgerigars are mainly green, with a yellow head and chin. They also have violet-blue patches on the cheeks. The tail is blue. Green, yellow and blue are the major colors of captive budgies, which may also have some white plumage, especially on the head and wings. Cocks can be distinguished from hens by the color of the cere. This is the fleshy area above the beak. The cock's cere is blue, the hen's brown.

Several distinctive color varieties have been developed over the years. They are named after the main body color and other characteristics. The name Opaline White-flighted Cobalt, for example, means that the body plumage is a vivid cobalt blue. "Opaline" means that the wing pattern is black mixed with the body color (in this case, blue). "White-flighted" indicates that the flight feathers are white.

Two of the most distinctive budgie varieties are the all-white Albino and the buttercup-yellow Lutino. They have no body markings, and red eyes.

PARROTS FOR PETS
When it comes to talking, parrots can outshine budgerigars. In the wild, parrots are found throughout all the tropical and sub-tropical forests of the world. Many species are available as cage birds, but generally they are not suited for such a life.

Parrots must only be purchased if it can be proved that they were bred in captivity. The trade in wild species

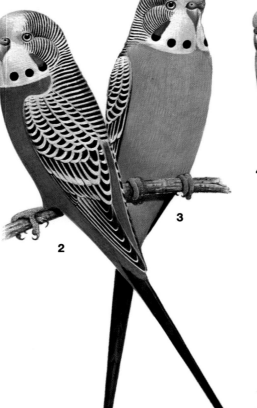

▲ ▶ **Plumage colors among varieties of budgerigar** Dutch Recessive Pied Yellow-faced Skyblue (hen) (1). Violet Cobalt (cock) (2). Gray (cock) (3). Australian Dominant Banded Pied Gray (cock) (4). Australian Dominant Pied Opaline Dark Green (cock) (5). Lacewing Yellow (hen) (6). Lutino (hen) (7). Opaline White-flighted Cobalt (cock) (8). Crested Skyblue (cock) (9). Tufted Green (hen) (10).

▼ Wild budgerigars flock in their thousands at a water hole near Alice Springs in central Australia. They move across the country in great flocks, following the rains.

is often cruel, and several kinds of parrot are close to extinction because of the pet trade.

The African gray is probably the best talker. It is nearly all gray, except for a bright red tail. The Amazon parrots of South America are also good talkers. They are mainly green, often with yellow on the head and patches of red and orange elsewhere.

Also natives of the Amazon region are the macaws, the largest and among the most colorful of all parrots. From beak to tail, they can measure nearly 3ft, over twice as big as the Amazons.

Even more vividly colored than the macaws, to which they are related, are the much smaller conures, also from South America. The bright red-orange-yellow Sun species is one of the finest. Smaller still (up to about 8in) are the South American Bee bee parrots, or parrotlets. Popular is the Canary-winged bee bee, which has yellow wing feathers.

▼Parrots can make nice pets, but need constant care for their entire lives of up to 50 years.

PIGEONS

For the past 16 days the male and female pigeons have taken turns sitting on the two eggs in the nest. Now the eggs are hatching. Soon the blind, naked squabs have their beaks wide open, craving for food. The parents thrust their beaks into those of the squabs and bring up partly digested food mixed with "milk." The milk is a nourishing liquid produced in their crops. The youngsters thrive, soon opening their eyes and growing feathers. In a little over 2 weeks they are ready to fly and live independently.

PIGEONS (1 domesticated species)

■ **Diet:** seeds, green food, scraps of animal and plant food.

○ **Breeding:** 2 eggs; incubation 16-17 days. Nests built on rock shelves, on cliffs or ledges, or in caves.

Distribution: domesticated and feral populations found worldwide except in hot deserts, polar regions, dense forests and on the highest mountains.

Breeds: several hundred breeds and many more varieties.

Size: length about 13in; domestic forms longer.

Color: most flying breeds and feral populations gray, black and white; fancy breeds many colors, including white, black, red, brown and gold.

Lifespan: up to about 8 years in captivity; often longer for feral populations.

Species mentioned in text:
Collared dove (*Streptopelia decaocto*)
Domesticated pigeon (*Columba livia*)
Stock dove (*C. oenas*)
Wood pigeon (*C. palumbus*)

Pigeons are usually seen in the greatest numbers in city squares and parks. They are often tame enough to be fed by hand. These are feral pigeons, descendants of domesticated birds that a long time ago escaped and then lived in the wild.

SEVERAL DIFFERENT GUISES
Domesticated pigeons are bred in many different colors. After a few generations in the wild, however, feral birds all tend to change back to the color of their wild ancestor, the Rock dove. This bird is still found in Europe, Asia and Africa. It has mainly slate-gray plumage, with two black bars on the wings. The rump is white.

In country areas the pigeons seen in parks may be not only feral domesticated pigeons, but also very similar looking birds of three different wild species of the same genus, *Columba*.

One is the Stock dove, which has a gray rump and only short black bars on the wings. The second is the Collared dove, so called because of the black band on the back of the neck. The third is the Wood pigeon, a bigger bird, with a length of about 16in from beak to tip of tail. It has white patches on the neck and on the wings, which show up in flight.

FOR CEREMONY AND SCIENCE
Rock doves might well have been the first birds to be domesticated, in the Middle East some 5,000 years ago. They were kept for ceremonies and sacrifices in the temples. They were also raised for meat.

Pigeons are still sometimes bred for meat today. The young pigeons, known as squabs, are marketed when they are about 1 month old.

Scientists also find pigeons useful, particularly when carrying out studies in learning and behavior. The birds are subjected to tests in which they have to respond to certain, usually visual, clues. They do so by pecking at any one of a number of keys, for example. When they get an answer correct, they are rewarded by food.

Pigeons perform so well in such experiments that some scientists believe that pigeons are more intelligent than any other animals except dogs, dolphins and primates.

FANCYING PIGEONS
Most pigeons today, however, are kept as a hobby. Pigeon fanciers may race their birds or exhibit them at

▼ On a stone ledge, a feral pigeon looks after her nest.

▲A pure-white Fantail shakes water from its plumage after a bath. Fantails are among the most spectacular of the fancy breeds of pigeons because of the way they display their magnificent tail.

shows. Over the years, hundreds of breeds have been developed.

Pigeons are easy to breed. Although the brood size is small (two), they can raise several broods a year. Selective breeding is made easier by the fact that, once paired, a male and female will remain together for many years, maybe for life. This happens even when, as is usual, the pair are part of a very large flock.

PIGEON POST

Most pigeons are able to find their way back home when released a few miles away from their loft, or house. Over several years, some birds have been selectively bred to bring out this homing instinct. The result is the homing pigeon, which can find its way back home over distances of hundreds of miles.

Homing pigeons were once used to carry messages, which were placed inside capsules attached to their legs. Communication by pigeons has been used in wartime for hundreds of years and even as recently as World War II. In the 1800s, pigeons were often used to carry messages when the telegraph broke down. At that time, too, pigeon racing began, first in Belgium, then in Britain and the United States.

BY CLOCK AND COMPASS

How homing pigeons find their way through the skies was once a puzzle. Now scientists have shown by experiments that the birds use two methods to point them in the right direction.

On clear, sunny days, the pigeons navigate by the Sun. From their internal "clock," they can tell the time of the day since they know precisely where the Sun should be in the sky at any particular moment. From this they work out, with great accuracy, in which direction their loft lies.

When the sky is overcast, pigeons use the Earth's magnetism to help them find their way. They seem to have little magnets inside the brain, which act like a compass to sense the direction of the Earth's magnetic field. From this they can work out the "compass bearing" of their loft and fly towards it.

The Sun and the Earth's magnetism will not as a rule take a pigeon in a straight line to its loft. They will guide it in the general direction until it gets close enough to recognize its surroundings. It does this not only by sight, but also by smell.

TUMBLERS AND ROLLERS

As well as the homing racers, there are two other interesting pigeon breeds. They each have a distinctive method of flying. One is the Tumbler. This has an inherited brain disorder which prevents it from flying normally. On

▼ **Variation in plumage and behavior among pigeon breeds** The Muffled White-side Tumbler (1) has long leg feathers and a characteristic tumbling flight. The Red Carrier (2) has white wattles and rosettes around the eyes. Black Maltese (3). The Powdered Silver Fantail (4) puts on a typical display. The Silesian Pouter (5), with neck puffed out. Egyptian Swift (6). Bronze Grazzi (7). The Baldhead Birmingham Roller (8) is named for the rolls it performs while it is flying.

its flight, the Tumbler climbs high into the air and then tumbles downwards. It often performs loops as it descends.

The Roller is another acrobat. It usually flies first in a circle for some time. Then it goes into a roll, throwing its head backwards as it does so.

▼Racing pigeons are released from their boxes all at the same time at the beginning of a race.

ALL PUFFED UP

Many other breeds of pigeon have been selectively bred to bring out particular features of behavior. The Pouters, for example, are birds that puff out the neck like a balloon. They do this by filling special sacs with air.

Fantails are also spectacular. They have as many as 30 tail feathers, more than twice the normal number. They spread these out in a fan, similar to a peacock. At the very same time, they throw out the breast and hold the head right back against the neck.

The Barb and Carrier are two other breeds of fancy pigeons that have striking features. They have fleshy wattles, or growths of skin around the beak, which look something like berries. Even more extraordinary are the fleshy rosettes around the eyes.

Among birds with unusual plumage is the Frillback. It has a band of curly feathers around the body.

GOLDFISH AND KOI

Two thirsty pet dogs lap at the garden pond. Within seconds, they have attracted the goldfish, which mill around just a few inches away from the dogs' noses. The goldfish know this is their feeding time. They are always fed after the dogs have been taken for a walk, and they have come to associate the drinking dogs with food. The dogs' owner scatters a handful of pellet food on to the surface of the water, and the fish gulp it down avidly.

The goldfish is among the world's most popular pets, and it is easy to see why. It is easy and cheap to look after. In an aquarium it can be kept indoors anywhere. In a pond outdoors it is hardy enough to survive the cold of winter, even when the water ices over.

ORIENTAL ORIGINS

Goldfish are closely related to both the Common carp and the Crucian carp. Carp have been kept in ponds by the Chinese for at least 2,000 years. They were first farmed for food. The koi is the domesticated form of the Common carp.

The ancestors of today's goldfish were probably red-gold individuals found among the wild goldfish of China, which are usually a dull olive-gray color. Fishermen may have kept these more attractive fish as pets. Over the centuries the golden fish have been bred into many different varieties. Goldfish came to the West from Japan, arriving in Europe in the 1700s and in North America in the 1800s.

Goldfish breed once a year. The males chase the females, which have become swollen with eggs. They keep bumping the females to make them release the eggs. The males release their milt (sperm) to bring about fertilization.

GOLDFISH AND KOI
(*2 species*)

◩ **Diet:** algae, insects, daphnia, bloodworms, dried food.

◯ **Breeding:** spawning takes place once a year, usually in late spring.

Distribution: worldwide in home aquaria and ponds.

Breeds: more than 150 varieties of goldfish and koi.

Size: length: goldfish up to about 12in in ponds; koi up to 40in.

Color: goldfish: gold, often with white and black patches; some breeds black; koi: multicolored, gold, red, blue, black, white.

Lifespan: goldfish: up to 30 years in ponds; koi: 30-200 years.

Species mentioned in text:
Common carp and koi (*Cyprinus carpio*)
Crucian carp (*Carassius carassius*)
Goldfish (*C. auratus*)

LIONHEADS AND VEILTAILS

Common goldfish come in a range of colors – silver, white, brown and gold, sometimes with dark markings. The young are pale at first, but gain more color as they grow.

The Shubunkin is a variety that has the same kind of body shape as the goldfish, but its body is commonly covered with gray, gold, red or blue patches, with black markings. The Comet is another popular breed. It is the same color and body shape as the Common goldfish, but grows longer fins and tail.

Long tails are a feature of some of the other varieties of fancy goldfish, which are aquarium rather than pond fish. The Fantail has a double tail held out like a fan. The long double tail of the Veiltail hangs down like a veil.

The Lionhead and Oranda are two varieties that have a growth like a raspberry over the head. The Black Moor is a striking all-black fish with long fins and protruding eyes. The Bubble-eye has large balloon-like sacs under the eyes, which wave about when the fish is swimming.

COLORFUL KOI

Colored varieties of the Common carp have been cultivated in Japan for centuries. However, the selective breeding that resulted in the present-day koi, or Rainbow carp (Nishiki-goi), only began there 100 years ago.

Koi are now becoming increasingly popular in the United States, where American-bred koi are a common pond fish in the warmer states, such as California. American koi tend to be somewhat smaller than Japanese koi, but are equally as colorful. In Europe, koi breeding is not so successful because of the climate. Most koi are imported from Japan or California.

▼To appreciate fully the color of koi, they should be viewed from the top and kept in water that is crystal clear.

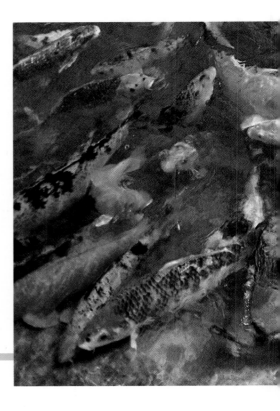

◄**Varieties of common and fancy goldfish** The colorful Shubunkin (1) is nearly as hardy as the Common goldfish and makes a pleasing contrast with it in the water. The Common goldfish (2) can live through even the coldest winters. Fancy goldfish such as the Lionhead (3), Veiltail (4), Bubble-eye (5) and Pompom (6) are less hardy and are better suited to the home aquarium. Their special features are also seen better there.

Among the standard colored koi types bred are the Kohaku (red and white), Kinutsuri (yellow and black) and Showa Sanke (red, white and black). There are two main body types, the Asian koi (Wagoi) and the broader-bodied German koi (Doitsu). Crossing color and body types gives varieties such as the Doitsu Showa Sanke and the Wagoi Kinutsuri.

To grow large and colorful, koi need to be kept in very clean, clear water. This keeps them healthy and makes them easy to see. Koi ponds therefore need to be large and require a good filtering system that can cope with large volumes of water. They are not practical for the small garden.

TROPICAL FISH

Two Siamese fighting fish are ready to spawn. The male is at the water's surface blowing bubbles, which cluster together to form a nest. Soon the female lays her eggs, and the male fertilizes them. Next, the male picks up an egg in its mouth, swims to the nest, and places the egg in a bubble. It repeats this until all the eggs are safe in the bubble nest.

▼ Male Siamese fighting fish are aggressive towards one another, and it is best to keep them apart. Constant fighting damages their long fins, as here.

TROPICAL FISH
(*about 200 freshwater and 20 sea water species available for the home aquarium*)

◪ Diet: algae, worms, water fleas, dried foods.

◗ Breeding: most species spawn, the male fertilizing eggs laid by the female; the eggs may hatch in a matter of days. Species such as the guppy and swordtail give birth to live young.

Distribution: kept worldwide as a hobby.

Size: length about 2in to 32in.

Color: virtually all colors of the rainbow; some bear spots or stripes.

Lifespan: up to about 5 years.

Species mentioned in text:
Barbs (*Barbus* species)
Black molly (*Poecilia sphenops*)
Blue angelfish (*Pomacanthus semicirculatus*)
Bronze catfish (*Corydoras aeneus*)
Cichlids (family Cichlidae)
Danios (e.g. *Brachydanio* species)
Gouramis (*Colisa* species)
Guppy (*Poecilia reticulata*)
Neon tetra (*Cheirodon axelrodi*)
Red platy (*Xiphophorus maculatus*)
Siamese fighting fish (*Betta splendens*)
Swordtail (*Xiphophorus helleri*)

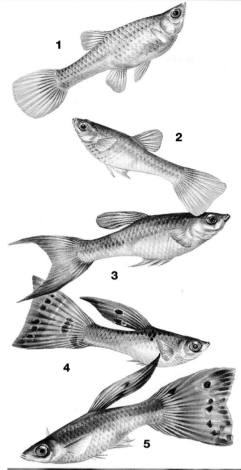

Keeping tropical fish, for instance the Siamese fighting fish, as a hobby started to become popular in the 1950s. Now it is practised on a wide scale. In the United States alone, over 16 million families keep tropical fish.

SELECTING THE FISH

Most popular for the home is a community aquarium, in which a selection of freshwater fish are kept. These must be chosen carefully so that they can live happily together. The aquarium must not be overcrowded. Care must also be taken to provide a suitable habitat for the particular fish selected, with regard to temperature of the water (usually 77°F), air supply, shelter and vegetation.

◄**Some varieties of guppy** The wild female (**1**) and male (**2**) are not very striking. Neither are the females of the domesticated guppies. However, from the age of about 3 months, the males become increasingly colorful and grow long fins. These are well displayed by the male Double Sword (**3**), Delta-tail (**4**) and Long Dorsal Veiltail (**5**).

At first, fish for the home aquarium were imported directly from tropical countries where they had been taken from the wild. A few South American countries still supply wild fish, but today 70 percent of freshwater tropical fish are bred in fish farms, particularly in Hong Kong, Thailand and Singapore. These farms raise not only Far Eastern breeds, but also breeds originally from South America.

The fish bred at farms are less hardy and have a shorter lifespan than the same species taken from the wild. However, taking any fish from the wild, particularly marine species, will reduce the population and affect the environment. The practice is discouraged by most conservation bodies.

THE LIVE-BEARERS

The guppy is one of the most popular tropical fish. It gives birth to live and

▼These Bronze catfish are natives of tropical fresh waters in Trinidad and Venezuela. They have whisker-like feelers on their lips.

▲ Modern techniques of maintaining water quality now make it possible to keep marine fish, such as this angelfish, in home aquaria. However, taking fish from the wild should be discouraged.

fully formed young. Guppies are very prolific breeders. In their native South America, they are known as millions fish because they produce so many young. The males of the species become increasingly colorful as they grow older. The females stay drab.

Both sexes of the Red platy are brightly colored, mainly in red and yellow. Males and females can be distinguished by the anal fin, which is rounded in the female and pointed in the male. The swordtail is also highly colored. It is named for the long curved lower end of its tail, which can be as long as its body. Swordtail varieties are usually red and green. Those with black fins are popularly known as wagtails.

The most striking of the molly species is the Black molly, which is the only all-black fish there is. The sailfin variety is noted for its tall dorsal fin.

THE EGG-LAYERS

Among the most popular species of egg-layers are the tetras, barbs, Siamese fighting fish, danios and cichlids. They all reproduce by spawning. The female lays its eggs in the water and then the male fertilizes them. The species differ in what happens to the eggs afterwards.

The danios, for example, just scatter the eggs at random and lose interest afterwards. The tetras and barbs lay adhesive eggs, which stick to the leaves of the aquarium plants. The cichlids lay adhesive eggs on flat stones that the breeding pair have thoroughly cleaned. When the eggs have hatched, one of the parents (usually the male) shepherds them in a group for safety.

BLOWING BUBBLES

By far the most interesting breeding behavior, however, is demonstrated by the Siamese fighting fish and the gouramis. They are bubble-nesters, which place their eggs in a nest of bubbles that they blow at the surface.

Siamese fighting fish are a particularly graceful species, slow-swimming and with long, flowing fins. They have a special organ for breathing air, which they take in gulps at the surface. This also allows them to blow bubbles for their nest. Another feature of the species is that it has long pelvic fins, which act like primitive feelers. The gouramis have these fins too.

▶ Tetras, such as these Neon tetras from pools in the jungle areas between Peru and Brazil, include some of the most colorful of all tropical fish.

CATTLE

It is mid-afternoon in a small town in India. A car is driving along the dusty main street. It makes slow progress, picking its way through the sauntering pedestrians, who don't move until the last second. But other obstructions don't move at all. They are the cows lying around chewing their cud. They must be avoided at all costs because they are sacred. Hindus, who make up most of the Indian population, revere the cow as a symbol of Mother Earth. And for good reason. They have depended on cattle for their livelihood for thousands of years. Cattle provide milk and are used as draft animals. But they are never slaughtered for meat.

India is the world's leading cattle-producing country, with about 200 million head. This represents about one-sixth of the world total. The Indian's view of the cow as a religious object harks back to when cattle were first domesticated 9,000 years ago.

Cattle were used to pull carts in religious ceremonies. Then they became more commonly used as draft animals, for example, for pulling the plow. Only later did they become a source of milk and meat. In Africa and Asia in particular, the use of cattle as draft animals still continues.

ORIGINS IN AFRICA

There appear to have been two early ancestors of today's main breeds of cattle, one large with long horns, and one small with short horns. In Europe, a wild breed of the large cattle existed until the 1600s. Called the aurochs, it was a massive beast that stood up to 7ft high at the shoulders, with long, curved horns.

Long-horn and short-horn cattle were both domesticated in ancient Egypt. So was another type, which had a fleshy hump on the withers (ridge between the shoulder blades). This was the ancestor of today's zebu breeds, noted for their resistance to tropical heat and diseases.

CATTLE TYPES

The term cattle covers cows (females), bulls (males) and also their offspring, calves. A heifer is a young cow that has not yet been mated. A bullock, or steer, is a male that has been castrated. Cattle are sometimes called oxen, but this name also refers to other members of the family Bovidae, such as the Water buffalo and yak.

In most countries cattle are raised for their meat and milk. Selective breeding over the centuries has resulted in specialist breeds suited to either meat production (beef breeds) or milk (dairy breeds). Other breeds have been developed as dual-purpose cattle, which provide milk as well as good-quality meat.

Hides are an important by-product of cattle farming, being used for making leather. Other products are fats, gelatine, glues and bone meal.

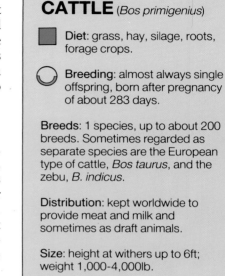

CATTLE (*Bos primigenius*)

■ Diet: grass, hay, silage, roots, forage crops.

● Breeding: almost always single offspring, born after pregnancy of about 283 days.

Breeds: 1 species, up to about 200 breeds. Sometimes regarded as separate species are the European type of cattle, *Bos taurus*, and the zebu, *B. indicus*.

Distribution: kept worldwide to provide meat and milk and sometimes as draft animals.

Size: height at withers up to 6ft; weight 1,000-4,000lb.

Color: varies with breed; black, gray, white, cream, brown, red.

Lifespan: up to 40 years, but few live beyond 20 years.

▼Ankole cattle grazing on the African savannah. They have the most enormous horns, 3ft or more long and often over 6½ft between the tips.

CHEWING IT OVER

Cattle are ruminants, with a special kind of stomach that enables them to digest grass and the other plant material they feed on. The stomach has four chambers. When a cow first swallows food, it passes into the first and largest chamber, known as the rumen. It is partly digested before being returned to the mouth as "cud." The cow chews the cud until it is thoroughly broken down before swallowing it again. This time it passes into each of the other chambers of the stomach and is completely digested.

Grazing cattle cannot bite off grass because they have no suitable teeth. A cow has eight incisors (cutting teeth) in the front of its lower jaw, but none in the upper. It grazes by grasping the grass with its rough tongue and then tearing it off with a rapid movement of the head. It chews with its back molars, 12 to each jaw.

RAISING BEEF

Beef cattle have been bred to have a wide, sturdy body, with plenty of flesh on the back and hindquarters. Among leading beef breeds are the Hereford and the Charolais. Herefords are the breed associated with the great cattle ranches of the American West. They thrive on poor grazing land. Charolais are exceptionally well-muscled and gain weight fast. One of the heftiest beef animals is the Santa Gertrudis, a humped breed.

In the American West and the open plains of Australia, beef cattle are ranched. They are left to roam by themselves for most of the year. The cattle ranches or stations can cover vast areas. The biggest of all is the Anna Creek station in South Australia, which covers an area of more than 11,500 sq mi, quarter the size of New York State! There, cattle herds may number tens of thousands of animals.

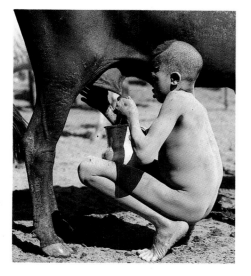

▲In a village street in southern Sudan a boy milks a cow.

▼The cow suckling the calf is a Friesian, one of the best milk producers. The bull is a Charolais, an excellent beef breed.

►Bali cattle haul the plow in a waterlogged rice-field. They are domesticated varieties of the banteng, a wild cattle from South-east Asia.

◄▼Some breeds of beef cattle The Texas Longhorn (1) is found in the western United States. It came originally from Texas, Mexico and New Mexico. The English Longhorn (2) has a red coat, with white lines along the back and tail. The Hereford (3), named for the British county from which it came, is the world's leading beef breed. The Limousin (4), from France, is found mainly there and in North America. It is economical to feed and has a high growth rate.

Elsewhere, beef herds are raised like dairy cattle, on pastureland on smaller farms. They may also be raised intensively; thousands of animals are kept in fenced enclosures and fed carefully calculated quantities of feed. They put on weight rapidly and are ready for market in less than a year.

In the tropics, there is now considerable environmental concern as great areas of natural forest are being felled to create pastureland for cattle.

DAIRY CATTLE

Dairy cattle are more lightly built than beef cattle, but have a broad rib-cage. They have well-developed udders, which hold the milk. Before it can give milk, a cow has to bear a calf. In most dairy herds these days, cows are not mated with a bull. They are made pregnant by artificial insemination. In this method, the semen from a bull is introduced artificially into the cow.

▲A herd of cattle being driven in Brazil. The breed is Nellore, a type of zebu. The cattle have the typical hump and long face of zebus.

▲Two breeds for a hot climate The Santa Gertrudis (1), a sanga breed farmed for beef on a large scale in Texas. It is a modern breed, derived from zebu stock. Its hump is not as prominent as that of the Kankrej (2), which is a straight zebu breed. The Kankrej came from the state of Gujarat in India. In that country it is widely used as a draft animal.

After a cow has given birth, it continues to give milk for about 9 to 10 months. To ensure a continual supply, farmers arrange for their cows to calve once a year. On average, good milking cows give about 3 gallons of milk a day. They are milked twice, first in the early morning then again in the late afternoon.

The breeds that give the most milk are the Friesians and Holsteins, both originally from the Netherlands and northern Germany. Every year each cow can produce 1,580 gallons.

BREEDS FOR HOT CLIMATES

The kinds of cattle familiar in the temperate climates of the West, such as Friesians and Herefords, would not survive in the tropical and sub-tropical climates of, say, Africa and Asia. They could not withstand the heat, and they would quickly succumb to pests and diseases. The cattle raised in vast numbers in these climates are of the humped zebu type. They have a longer, narrower skull than ordinary cattle and long drooping ears.

Zebus are native to India and are found in largest numbers there. Most animals are mixtures of the 26 or so zebu breeds. But some are purer bred. The very best draft animals are the Kankrej, and the best milk-producers, the Red Sindhi.

Along with two other Indian zebus, the Kankrej has been introduced into Brazil and a number of other Latin American countries. The Brazilian and Indian zebus provided the breeding stock for the Brahman, first bred in the southern United States and now raised throughout the tropics and sub-tropics for beef.

There are many zebu crosses with humpless cattle, which can also tolerate hot climates. Known as sangas, they include one of the most distinctive of all cattle breeds, the Ankole of East Africa. It is noted for its incredibly large horns, but it is valued more as a status symbol than as a farm animal.

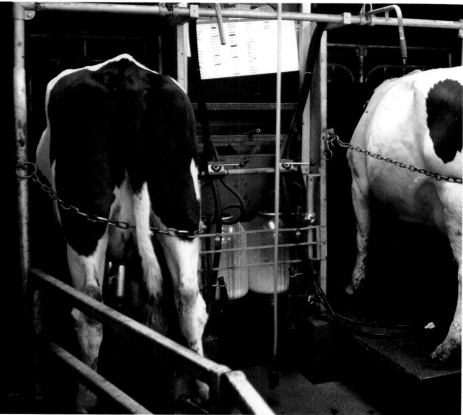

▲**Some breeds of dairy cattle** The Brown Swiss (1), from Switzerland, is used to grazing high up in the mountains. It is now found in other mountainous countries, such as Peru. The Jersey (2), from the Channel Islands, is noted for its rich, creamy milk. The Normandy (3), of north-west France, is descended from Viking cattle. The Friesian (4), originally from the Netherlands, is now found worldwide. The Dairy Shorthorn (5) was bred in north-west England.

▶Friesian cows being milked in a milking parlor. Here milking is done by machine. Suction cups are fitted over the teats, and the milk is drawn off in a rhythmic squeezing and sucking action. Milk from each cow is fed into a separate container so that records can be kept of the cow's milk yield.

WATER BUFFALOS

Two swamp buffalos have been hard at work since early in the morning. It is now nearly noon, and the heat is becoming unbearable. But their working day is ended. The farmer unharnesses them from the cart, and they head immediately for the deep mud at the edge of the stream. They stir up the cool mud with their massive horns, and roll blissfully in it. They wallow there contented until the Sun loses its murderous heat.

The Water buffalo was domesticated before 2500 BC by people of the Indus civilization, who lived in the region we now call Pakistan. About 1,300 years ago it was introduced to the Mediterranean region. Herds were established in Italy. and Egypt, where they are still important farm animals.

It is in tropical and sub-tropical Asia, however, that Water buffalos are found in the largest numbers. This is where rice is the major crop. Water buffalos are ideal animals to help in cultivating it. They are more than

willing to plow and to harrow the ground after it has been flooded. Wallowing in the water is in any case their favorite pastime!

WALLOWING
Water buffalos must be allowed to wallow in water or be sprayed with it in the heat of the day. This is because

► Water buffalo bulls hauling a massive load of logs from the forest. To haul larger loads, a team of up to eight buffalo, or buffalo and oxen, are used.

▼ Two teams of Water buffalo at work plowing a flooded rice paddy field in Java. They are perfectly at home up to their bellies in water.

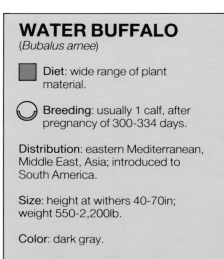

WATER BUFFALO
(*Bubalus arnee*)

■ Diet: wide range of plant material.

◑ Breeding: usually 1 calf, after pregnancy of 300-334 days.

Distribution: eastern Mediterranean, Middle East, Asia; introduced to South America.

Size: height at withers 40-70in; weight 550-2,200lb.

Color: dark gray.

Lifespan: about 20 years on average.

they have fewer sweat glands and generally a poorer system of heat control than cattle. Wallowing also helps keep away ticks and flies.

Altogether there are about 130 million Water buffalos in the world. This figure includes feral animals – those that have returned to the wild. One of the largest feral populations is found in northern Australia, around Darwin. It numbers some 250,000 head and causes serious damage to vegetation. There are a few genuine wild Water buffalos in the grass jungles of Nepal.

A SOURCE OF MILK AND MEAT

Water buffalos are utilized as draft animals in every country where they are farmed. Many also provide the farmers with milk and meat.

In India, Water buffalos provide 70 percent of all the nation's milk, and special milking varieties have been developed. In Egypt, too, they are more important than cattle as milk producers. They produce more milk, and it is much richer in nutrients.

Water buffalo meat is good to eat and is particularly lean. Their milk contains more solids than cows' milk and makes excellent cheese. The well-known Italian cheese mozzarella is made from buffalo milk.

DIFFERENT TYPES

The Water buffalos raised mainly for their milk are a type known as river buffalos. They prefer to wallow in clear water. They are to be found mostly in northern India, the Middle

East and the eastern Mediterranean region, particularly in Turkey.

Swamp buffalos are another type, which by contrast like to wallow in the mud. They are raised mainly as draft animals and for their meat. They do not produce much milk.

Swamp buffalos are found in China, southern India, and other parts of eastern Asia. In the Philippines they are known as carabaos. They are noted for their massive upturned horns, which are shaped like sickles, and can span as much as 5ft. The horns of river buffalos are set closer to the head and are often swept down.

Many Water buffalos are a mixture of the two types and have no special breeding line. They are called desi and are used mainly for draft.

SHEEP

On a day in early summer, in the Béarn region of France, a shepherd leads his flock of some 300 sheep across a river and up on to the mountain slopes. He tends his sheep using the traditional trans-humance system of moving herds great distances between winter and summer pasture so as not to let the animals overgraze the land.

After cattle, sheep are the farm animals kept in the largest numbers. The total world population is over 1,100 million. More than 140 million are raised in Australia alone, where the biggest flocks can be found.

HORNED AND HORNLESS

Sheep were domesticated, perhaps more than 10,000 years ago, in the region once known as the Fertile Crescent. This includes the present-day countries of Israel, Lebanon, Syria, Turkey and Iraq. By about 6,000 years ago sheep were being farmed all over Europe and Asia. The Spanish introduced sheep to the Americas in the 1500s. They were brought to Australia after the first convict settlement was set up there in 1788.

The male sheep are called rams, the females ewes, and the young lambs. In some breeds both the ram and the ewe have horns. In others only the ram is horned. In a few breeds both sexes are polled (hornless). A sheep's horns tend to grow outwards from the head as opposed to a goat's, which grow upwards. Rams' horns often grow in a spiral, like a corkscrew. In almost all sheep breeds the animals have two horns. The ancient Manx Loghtan breed unusually has four.

▶A shepherd boy with a flock of Karakuls in Namibia. These sheep are raised for milk and the pelts of the lambs.

RAISING SHEEP

Sheep may be raised in a number of ways. Nomadic tribes in Africa and Asia herd them in much the same way as they have for centuries, moving them constantly in search of suitable grazing. Sheep may also be raised on farms in fenced pastureland and fed when necessary on hay, roots, grain or commercial pellet food.

By far the largest numbers of sheep, however, are raised on the open range, as on the great sheep stations of Australia. They are able to make use not only of grass, but also of other native vegetation. They are left to their own devices for most of the year. This makes them easy and cheap to raise. Yet, if large numbers of sheep are allowed to roam freely over grassland

SHEEP (Ovis aries)

■ Diet: grass, weeds, crops, hay.

◎ Breeding: 1 or 2 offspring, after pregnancy of 143-159 days.

Breeds: 1 species, up to about 300 breeds and varieties. Classified as separate species are the urial (*Ovis orientalis*), the mouflon (*O. musimon*) and the argali (*O. ammon*).

Distribution: worldwide, except in extremes of climate.

Size: height at withers 16-34in; weight 55-330lb (males), 45-230lb (females).

Color: usually white, sometimes with black face and ears.

Lifespan: up to 13 years.

for prolonged periods, the vegetation is soon stripped from the land and cannot readily regrow. In many parts of the developing world especially, in this way sheep are now causing increasing environmental problems.

Every few weeks or so, sheep are rounded up for shearing and dipping. Rounding them up is not too much of a problem because sheep have a particularly strong herd instinct and tend to keep together in flocks.

Dipping is a way of controlling sheep ticks and other parasites, such as lice and mites, which cause a disease called sheep scab. The process involves dipping the sheep in a trough of insecticide twice a year. Sheep can also suffer from foot rot and from internal parasites, for example worms.

MULTI-PURPOSE ANIMALS

Meat and wool are the main products obtained from sheep. The wool is generally removed once a year by shearing. Sheepskins with the wool attached are made into warm clothing and they also have uses in industry. In ancient times the skin was used to make parchment for writing.

In some countries even the dung of sheep is useful. Nomadic peoples dry it for use as fuel. Elsewhere, sheep are grazed on land to fertilize it.

SHEEP'S EYES

In Western countries, most sheep meat is eaten as lamb. Lambs are sent for slaughter when they are 3 to 8 months old. The meat of mature sheep, often called mutton, is not as tender as lamb and is generally used for stewing rather than roasting.

Most parts of the sheep are eaten. The brains and eyes are considered to be delicacies in some countries. The stomach and guts are used as casing for sausages and black (blood) puddings. In parts of central and eastern Africa, the blood of the living sheep is drunk by some nomads, usually from a cut above the eye.

HAIR SHEEP

The only sheep kept almost entirely for meat production are the so-called hair breeds. They have a sparse fleece of coarse fibers, with little or no underfur. Similar sheep appear in ancient Egyptian pictures and bas reliefs dating back 5,000 years.

Hair sheep are raised in largest numbers in tropical and sub-tropical regions, including Africa, southern India, the Caribbean and nearby Central America. The West African Dwarf is a black-and-white hair sheep widely raised in Africa. The ram has a thick mane and ruff, like the males of some of the other hair breeds.

◄Using modern electric shears, a skilled sheep-shearer can remove the fleece from over 90 sheep in an hour!

▼These wild sheep, called mouflons, are found in southern Europe and parts of Asia. The mouflon is thought to be the main ancestor of modern sheep breeds.

FAT TAILS AND RUMPS

The tails of the hair breeds are long and thin. They could not be more different from the tails of the equally ancient fat-tailed or fat-rumped sheep breeds. These breeds are so-called because they store fat in their short, broad tail or rump. In extreme cases the tail can account for up to one-fifth of the carcass weight. It is considered a delicacy and is usually sold separately.

Among fat-tailed breeds are the Karakul and Hu. The Karakul came originally from Turkey and Iran, but it is now farmed throughout western Asia and in south-west Africa. The Hu originated from, and is now widely farmed in, eastern China. The lambs are slaughtered when only 2 or 3 days old for their pelts of tightly curled wool. Those of the Karakul are known as Astrakhan or Persian lamb.

SELECTIVE BREEDING

Down and longwool sheep breeds originated in Britain, where systematic breeding began in the mid-to-late 1700s. The object was to improve existing breeds so that they produced a better carcass for meat production.

▼A variety of sheep breeds The Soay (1) is an ancient breed from the St Kilda Islands of Scotland. It is thought to resemble the sheep kept thousands of years ago. The Sudanese (2) is an attractive-looking desert-hair breed found in Africa. It has a distinctive brown and white fleece. The Dalesbred (3) is a hardy highland breed with very springy wool, much used for making tweed cloth and carpets. The Mongolian (4) is one of the fat-tailed sheep, raised in its native Mongolia and China.

By selectively breeding the long-fleeced native sheep, the modern longwool breeds developed. They include the Leicester, Wensleydale, Lincoln, and Kent or Romney Marsh, named after the regions in which they became established. From the native shortwool sheep, the so-called down breeds were developed. They include the Southdown and Suffolk which are used for siring lambs for slaughter.

FINE-WOOLLED MERINOS

For wool production, all the merino breeds of sheep are supreme. They

▲These sheep are crosses of English longwool breeds. They are raised mainly for their meat.

◀▼Some merino, longwool and downs breeds The long-legged Arles Merino (1) was bred by crossing Spanish Merinos with sheep from the Arles region of France. The Ile de France (2) is a longwool breed from the Paris region. It was bred from French Rambouillets and English Leicesters. The Corriedale (3) of New Zealand is from merino and English longwool stock. The German Blackface (4) is a downs breed, obtained by crossing Hampshire and Oxford downs sheep from England.

1

2

3

4

produce a heavy fleece of the finest wool. Modern merino breeds developed from the Spanish Merino, which dates back at least to the 1100s. Spain jealously guarded its stock, and it was not until the late 1700s that Spanish Merinos spread throughout Europe. They were crossed with local sheep to develop new breeds.

German Merinos became particularly important at one stage. They formed the foundation stock for the Australian Merinos, which now produce a quarter of the world's wool. King Louis XVI established the French merino breed known as Rambouillet. Rambouillets have proved invaluable for improving other merino breeds. American Rambouillets were crossbred from French Rambouillets and German Merinos.

MILK AND CHEESE

Sheep are kept mainly for their wool and meat, but in some countries they are also valued for their milk. Sheep's milk is much richer than that of cows and goats. It contains over twice as much fat as cow's milk and 70 percent more protein.

Sheep's milk is produced in greatest quantities in India and France. It is not normally drunk, but made into such products as yoghurt and cheese. One of the best-known French cheeses, Roquefort, is made from sheep's milk.

In recent years specialist breeds have been developed to produce a higher milk yield. They include the Ostfriesisches Milchschaf which came originally from northern Germany. Crossbreeds of this with the Awassi are popular in Israel.

▶A ewe and its lamb. Lambs are born fully developed, and are able to run around only a few hours after leaving the womb.

GOATS

Up in the Atlas mountains of Morocco a goat is grazing on tufts of the tough wiry grass that grows sparsely in this Sun-baked scrubby landscape. Then it spies what looks like a particularly succulent bunch of leaves up in the branches of a stunted tree nearby. It tries to reach the bunch by standing on its hind legs, but it is not tall enough. So, with one bound, it leaps up into the branches. Keeping its balance with remarkable ease, it makes for the chosen leaves and happily eats its fill.

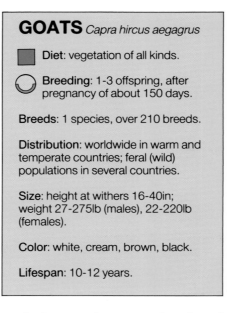

GOATS *Capra hircus aegagrus*

■ **Diet:** vegetation of all kinds.

◐ **Breeding:** 1-3 offspring, after pregnancy of about 150 days.

Breeds: 1 species, over 210 breeds.

Distribution: worldwide in warm and temperate countries; feral (wild) populations in several countries.

Size: height at withers 16-40in; weight 27-275lb (males), 22-220lb (females).

Color: white, cream, brown, black.

Lifespan: 10-12 years.

▲ A figurine from the ancient city of Ur, Mesopotamia (Iraq), which shows a goat climbing the Tree of Life.

▼ In the mountainous country of Nepal goats are useful as pack animals to carry supplies where there are no roads.

Goats are kept in enormous numbers throughout the world in dry, scrubby and mountainous regions. This is because they are able to survive on the sparsest vegetation, which most other animals, such as cattle and sheep, could not digest. Goats are particularly fond of woody vegetation, and their tough lips can cope even with the thorniest of bushes. In some regions goats have overgrazed the scanty plant-life, causing it to disappear.

The goat is a ruminant, with several stomachs to digest the tough material it eats. Like cows, goats "chew the cud," returning wads of partly digested food to their mouth for further chewing to help break it down.

The male goat is usually called a billy or a ram. The female goat is often called a nanny or doe. A young goat is called a kid until it is a year old.

SPOT THE DIFFERENCE
Goats may have been domesticated before sheep, but no one is sure. Certainly they were being herded 9,000 years ago. At first sight it is sometimes difficult to distinguish between some breeds of goat and sheep. But there are several basic differences between these two animals.

The horns of goats are flattish and grow straight up before curving outwards. Those of sheep grow out to the side and often curve like a corkscrew. Most goats have a beard, while sheep do not. Male goats are strong smelling because of scent glands they have beneath the tail. Sheep do not have this unpleasant "goaty" smell. And while sheep have a fine woolly coat, goats have a tough hairy one, though some have a kind of wool underneath.

Another difference between the two animals lies in their temperament. Goats are naturally very lively, inquisitive and independent. They

◀Goats love to eat the leaves of shrubs. They will even climb into the branches to reach the most tasty shoots. By overgrazing, goats can turn scrub vegetation to desert.

▼The Anglo-Nubian Goat is noted for its long, drooping ears. It is a hornless breed, farmed widely for its milk.

make good companions and pets. By comparison sheep appear to be quite docile and stupid.

GOATS AROUND THE WORLD

There are estimated to be 450 million goats in the world. This includes feral goats – those that have escaped into the wild – as well as farmed goats. Today's breeds of domesticated goats are thought to have descended from the wild goat, or bezoar (*Capra aegagrus*). This animal is still found today on Greek islands, in Turkey, the Middle East and other parts of Asia.

Nearly three-quarters of all goats are found in Africa and Asia. There they are kept as general-purpose animals, for their meat, milk, fiber and skin. In Europe, North America, Australia and New Zealand, though, goats are raised mainly as dairy animals.

PRODUCING MEAT AND MILK

Taken overall, more goats are kept for meat than for any other purpose. As much as 2 million tons of goat meat are eaten every year, mainly in Africa and Asia. It is very lean and has a pleasant flavor, similar to that of lamb, but it tends to be somewhat tougher.

Many of the goats that are raised for their meat are also milked. However, better milk yields are obtained from specialist milk breeds. The traditional milk breeds include the Tamnapari of India and the Mamber of the Near and Middle East.

In the late 1800s goat keepers in England crossed local breeds with goats brought over from the East, including one from Nubia, in northeast Africa. This led to the modern breed of lop-eared Anglo-Nubians,

which are now farmed in large numbers for their milk. On average, an Anglo-Nubian produces up to 210 gallons of milk a year, twice that of a Tamnapari.

The Saanens, which originally came from Switzerland, produce most milk. One Saanen in Australia has produced over 920 gallons of milk in a year, although the average is 260. Another Swiss breed, the Toggenburg, is also an excellent milk breed.

HELPING THE DIGESTION

Goat's milk is a nourishing food, which is pleasant to taste and easier to digest than cow's milk. It has a similar composition to cow's milk, and provides a useful alternative for people with digestive problems.

Goat's milk does not make good butter, but it does make excellent cheese. Both soft and hard cheeses are produced, particularly in France and other Mediterranean countries. Yoghurt is traditionally made in south-east Europe from goat's milk.

THE BEST FLEECE

Goat's hair has been used for making cloth for thousands of years. Two breeds in particular have been selectively bred to produce a fleece finer than any obtained from a sheep.

▶In the mountains of Afghanistan it is milking time for the family goats. They also provide meat and wool.

▼Here in Uganda goats share a drinking trough with a herd of cattle. The goats are raised for their meat and skins.

▲▶ **Breeds of goat kept for their milk**
The Nordic (1) comes from Norway, Sweden and Finland. The Anglo-Nubian (2) was first bred in England in the late 1800s from eastern stock. The Toggenburg (3) and Saanen (4) came originally from Switzerland. The black-and-white British Alpine (5).

One is the Angora (from the name Ankara, the capital of Turkey), an animal that usually has drooping ears and horns that have a right-angle twist in them. Their white fleece is long and hangs from the body in shiny ringlets. The Angora is sheared like a sheep, and can produce a fleece weighing as much as 11lb.

The fiber obtained from the fleece is known as mohair. The word comes from the Arabian word *mukhayyar*, meaning best fleece. Mohair is a silky fiber that takes dyes well. It is widely used for making lightweight suiting and fabrics of all kinds, from curtains to carpets. The finest cloth is made from the hair of young animals. The fibers are typically about 8in long.

Angora Goats, which are natives of central Asia, are now farmed on a large scale in Turkey, Texas, Argentina, Australia and Africa. South Africa is the world's largest producer of mohair.

COMFORTABLE CASHMERE

The other leading breed raised for fiber is the Cashmere. This goat has long, straight and twisted horns, and erect ears. It grows a coat of coarse outer hair, with soft downy fur underneath. The underfur is combed out or plucked when the animal molts. It is the fiber of this underfur that is valuable. It is called cashmere, or pashmina. It is the finest of all animal fibers used for textiles, with a fiber

thickness of less than 60 thousandths of an inch – microscopically thin!

WORTH ITS WEIGHT IN GOLD

The Cashmere Goat is named after Kashmir, one of the regions in central Asia where it originated. There are other breeds that produce a similar fiber. These include the Chungwei of China, the Kurdi of Iraq and the Don of Russia. The fiber is a by-product of animals raised mainly for their milk and meat.

Cashmere is the finest of all animal fibers, and makes up into fabrics of exceptional warmth and comfort. As many as five goats may be needed to produce enough fiber to make one sweater. For this reason cashmere clothes are expensive. The famous "ring shawls" brought to Europe from India by the Italian explorer Marco Polo in the late 13th century were so fine they could be passed through a wedding ring!

GOAT SKINS

Cashmere Goats also provide good-quality skins for leather manufacture. Leather is produced from most other breeds, which are kept mainly for milk or meat. The Red Sokoto of Nigeria is one of the few breeds kept primarily for their skin.

Goat skin produces leather of very high quality, including the famous Morocco, used for example to make gloves and for binding books. This was made originally in Morocco and southern Europe. Goat skins are also made into rugs the world over and into containers for carrying water and wine. It has been estimated that about 350,000 fresh goat skins are produced each year throughout the world.

▲ ▶ **Breeds of goat raised for their fiber, meat or skin** The Angora (1), prized for its lustrous coat. The Kambang Kabjang (2) is raised for its meat, mainly in South-east Asia. Another famous fiber breed is the Cashmere (3). The Red Sokoto (4) has a distinctive mahogany-colored coat. It is farmed for its skins, mainly in Nigeria. The West African Dwarf, or Pygmy (5), may stand only 16in high at the withers (shoulders). It is raised for meat.

▶ Sunlight picks out the lustrous hair of two Angora Goats. The twisted horns and horizontal ears are typical of this Asian breed.

PIGS

The large white pigs grunt excitedly in their sty as they hear the farmer coming to feed them. He empties a nourishing feed of corn and soybean meal into their trough, and they noisily begin to eat. But when they have eaten their fill, they stop. The expression "eating like a pig" to describe someone who overeats is not a good one, because pigs seldom gorge themselves. But the animals do get themselves dirty. They wallow in the mud to keep themselves cool because their tough skin does not have any sweat glands.

Almost 800 million pigs are now kept throughout the world. Nearly half of them are in Asia. Unlike other domesticated livestock, such as cattle, sheep and goats, pigs are a single-purpose breed. They are kept just for meat. Pig meat is eaten in two main forms: fresh, as pork, or cured (preserved), as bacon and ham.

Pigs also yield useful by-products. Their skins can be made into leather (pigskin), their fat yields lard used for cooking, and the bristles that cover the body can be made into brushes.

ON THE FARM

In many parts of Africa and Asia, pigs are kept by families for their own use. The animals are allowed to roam freely, feeding on roots, whole plants, worms and scraps. Elsewhere they are raised on farms, either in small numbers in sties, or in larger numbers in the fields or indoors in intensive schemes. When farmed intensively, hundreds of pigs are kept under cover in pens in a controlled environment. They are fed with carefully calculated amounts of feed so that they reach their market weight in the shortest possible time.

Pigs raised for pork are ready for market at up to about 155lb weight. In an intensive unit this weight can be reached when the animals are only about 3 months old. Such pigs are able to gain weight at the rate of up to 28 ounces a day. Pigs raised specifically for bacon are marketed when they are about 200 to 220lb in weight.

PIGS (*1 main species plus several others*)

Diet: very varied: grain, protein feeds such as soybean oil and fish meal, skimmed milk, plants, berries, fruit, worms.

Breeding: 6-16 offspring, after pregnancy of about 115 days.

Breeds: 87 recognized breeds and over 225 additional varieties.

Distribution: worldwide in warm and temperate climates.

Size: height up to 40in, weight 180-440lb.

Color: black, white, red.

Lifespan: over 15 years.

Species mentioned in text:
Babirusa (*Babyrousa babyrussa*)
Bearded pig (*Sus barbatus*)
Celebes wild pig (*S. celebensis*)
Domestic pig (*S. domestica*)
Wild boar (*S. scrofa*)

▶In the highlands of Papua New Guinea, Melpa tribesmen exchange pigs as part of a gift-giving ceremony.

PARENTS AND OFFSPRING

A pig has small eyes and poor eyesight, though its sense of smell is very good. Its "nose" is a leathery pad-like snout, which it uses to dig for roots (rooting). Pigs at pasture often have a ring fitted through the snout to stop them rooting and damaging the ground. The eyeteeth of a pig, especially the male, may develop into sharp tusks. In the wild these are used for rooting and fighting, but on farms they are usually clipped off.

A male pig is called a boar. A female is called a gilt before it has been mated, and a sow afterwards. Gilts are usually mated when they are about 7 to 8 months old. Sometimes they are put to the boar, but mostly semen from a boar is introduced artificially into a sow's reproductive system.

The sows farrow, or give birth, a little over 16 weeks later. As many as 25 young may be born in a litter. They are suckled by the sow for about 3 weeks. Just over a week later, the sow may be mated again.

ANCIENT AND MODERN BREEDS

The pig was domesticated about 9,000 years ago. The Wild boar was one of the principal wild ancestors of the

◀These striped piglets are the result of crossing a Tamworth breed sow and a Wild boar male.

▼Two domestic pigs from Vietnam. Oriental breeds like this were introduced into Europe in the 1800s.

European breeds of domestic pig. The first systematic attempts to improve pig breeds took place in England in the 1700s. Old English breeds were crossed with breeds from China.

One of the finest animals to result was the Large White. This breed has been the foundation of many modern breeds, not only in England, but also in continental Europe. In Denmark, for example, the Large White was crossed with the Landrace, the native Scandinavian pig. The outcome was the Danish Landrace, now one of the world's top breeds. Unlike the Large White, it has drooping ears. It gives a top-quality carcass with little fat.

▲ In the Perigord region of France, pigs are used to sniff out truffles, an underground fungus prized as a delicacy. Truffles often grow among the roots of oak trees.

◀▼ **Bacon breeds of pig** This Tamworth sow (1) is pregnant and is building a nest in which to farrow (give birth). The Tamworth is an ancient English breed, once in danger of extinction. Danish Landrace (sow) (2): an early 20th-century breed, which has Large White blood. A Large White boar (3) being threatened.

The Berkshire is another ancient English breed, which has been widely crossbred. The Poland China from America, for example, comes from Berkshire stock. Like the old breed, it is mainly black, with tail, feet and ears tipped with white. The Poland China differs from the Berkshire in having drooping ears.

WILD TYPES AND HYBRIDS

In many countries, pigs have escaped from captivity and reverted to the wild. Such feral pigs are now found in southern United States, where they are often called razorbacks because of their sharp, narrow back. They often cause damage to crops. Feral pigs cause a similar problem in Australia and New Zealand.

There are also large feral populations throughout Asia, where they are widely hunted for meat. Truly wild species, such as the Bearded pig and babirusa of South-east Asia, are also hunted. Another wild species of the region, the Celebes wild pig, has been domesticated throughout the Philippines, Sulawesi (formerly the Celebes) and neighboring islands.

▲ ▼ **Pork and lard breeds of pigs** British Saddleback sow (1); it is named for the pinkish-white "saddle" on its back. Andalusian (2): farmed in Spain and elsewhere in the Mediterranean region. Duroc boar (3) courting. The Duroc is a leading breed in the United States, improved recently by cross-breeding with the Tamworth. Berkshire (young sow, or gilt) (4): this black breed has white tips to the feet, tail and ears.

CHICKENS

It is just 3 weeks since the hen began to brood and incubate the clutch of eggs. Now she can hear the faint tapping as the chicks start to peck their way out of the shells. One by one, over the next day or so, the chicks emerge, wet and bedraggled at first, and cheep their way into the outside world. They dry into yellow fluffy bundles and bury themselves inside their mother's fluffed-out feathers.

▼A small flock of White Leghorns is let out of their house to feed in the early morning on a farm in Bresse, France.

CHICKENS (1 main species plus several others)

Diet: grain, protein meal (soybean, fish), food scraps, seeds, insects, worms.

Breeding: in the wild, clutches of 10-15 eggs, but domestic breeds continue laying, producing on average about 240 eggs a year; eggs take 21 days to hatch; most eggs now hatched in incubators.

Breeds: about 500 breeds and varieties.

Distribution: worldwide.

Size: weight 1 to 14lb. Depending on use, some birds are marketed before they reach full size and weight.

Color: varies widely; white, buff, black, red; plumage often iridescent. Males are usually more brightly colored than females.

Lifespan: several years (egg-layers).

Species mentioned in text:
Jungle fowl (*Gallus gallus*);
also *G. lafayettii*, *G. sonneratii* and *G. varius*

Domestic chickens are thought to have descended from the Jungle fowl, a bird that still lives in southern Asia. The cocks (males) of this species are orange-red and shiny greenish-black, while the hens (females) are a speckled brown for camouflage. The hens cackle and the cocks crow much like domesticated chickens.

Domestication probably first took place some 6,000 years ago. By Roman times chickens were being raised in western Europe. They were kept then as much for cock-fighting as for meat. Strangely enough, eggs were not eaten on a large scale until after 1800.

Today, some 7,000 million chickens are kept throughout the world. They provide nearly one-third of all the meat consumed. In the developing countries of Africa, Asia and South America, many families each keep a few chickens for their own use. They are of no particular breed and provide both meat and eggs.

In developed countries, however, breeds have been developed just for egg-laying or for meat production. Some are raised in the farmyard in the traditional way, but most are raised in huge numbers by intensive production methods.

BROILERS AND CAPONS

Chickens for meat are raised by the thousand indoors under carefully controlled conditions. They are fed a perfectly balanced diet so that they gain weight rapidly. They are usually marketed, as broilers, when they are about 8 weeks old and weigh 4½lb.

Capons are much older, heavier birds. They are males that have been castrated. This prevents their flesh becoming stringy as they grow older.

One of the commonest breeds used for meat production is a cross between female White Plymouth Rocks (originally from the United States) and male Cornish (originally from England). From the female line the birds get very rapid growth, for they make

▲These free-range chickens feed on any insects and worms they find and on seeds provided by the farmer.

▼A Silver Sebright cockerel. This is an ornamental breed of bantam, developed in England in the mid-1800s.

the most efficient use of feed. From the male line, they get a broad, heavily muscled body.

Other leading meat breeds are the New Hampshire Red and Wyandotte in the United States, and the Sussex in Britain and continental Europe.

THE EGG-LAYERS

Most chickens raised for egg-laying are also farmed by intensive methods in flocks of thousands. They are kept confined in small wire cages called batteries. Many people condemn this practice as inhumane, but it seems the only way of satisfying the huge consumer demand for eggs.

In a battery unit the temperature level is carefully controlled, and the length of the hens' day is regulated by switching artificial lighting on and off. This has the effect of keeping the hens laying over a much longer period than they would if they were influenced by seasonal changes in temperature and day length. Under such conditions hens lay up to 300 eggs per year.

The other method of raising hens is more traditional. It allows them to range freely on pasture and nest and lay in chicken houses. Many people consider the eggs of these hens are superior to those from battery hens, but they are more expensive.

About three out of every four hens raised commercially for eggs are Leghorns, originally from Italy. Improved

▶**Breeds of chicken** Except for the Ancona, Campine and Leghorn, they are dual-purpose breeds, suitable for meat and egg-production. Wyandotte **(1)** (U.S.), stands up to cold weather well. Welsummer **(2)** (Netherlands); this is a cockerel, the hens are brown. Ancona **(3)** (Italy). La Flèche **(4)** (France). Plymouth Rock **(5)** (U.S.), a famous breed that gains weight rapidly. Campine **(6)** (Belgium) is mostly kept for showing; this is the Golden variety. Rhode Island Red **(7)** (U.S.), another famous breed named for the U.S. state. Leghorn **(8)** (Italy), the foremost egg-laying breed. Barnvelder **(9)** (Netherlands); raised in Europe.

strains of this breed, notably the White Leghorn, were developed in England about a century ago. The tendency of the hens to brood was gradually bred out. Nowadays, Leghorns of every color are raised.

JUST FOR SHOW

Most chickens raised in the farmyard or commercially are hybrids. They are the result of cross-breeding. Pure, or standard, breeds are raised mainly for exhibition purposes at poultry shows. Each must conform to a set show standard. Some of the pure breeds exhibited, such as the Cornish, provide foundation stock for the poultry industry. The true ornamental breeds, however, are bred just for exhibition or as a hobby.

Many of the ornamental breeds came originally from the Far East. They include the Malay, Langshan, Brahma and Yokohama. The Yokohama is noted for its exceptionally long (up to 40in) tail feathers. One of the oldest ornamental breeds is the Old English Game. It is an agressive bird descended from the fighting cocks introduced to Britain by the Romans. One of the most striking ornamental chickens is the Polish, which has a large crest, a beard and also feathers on its face.

Miniature chickens of most breeds have also been developed. Called bantams, they sometimes weigh as little as 15 ounces. Some breeds have no full-size equivalent. They include the Sebright, Cochin and Japanese.

▼After three weeks in the incubator, the eggs are hatching. The chicks peck at the shell from the inside until it cracks.

▶In a large egg-laying battery, birds are kept in their thousands in a controlled environment, confined in small cages.

TURKEYS

The turkey tom is putting on an impressive display to woo the hen. It spreads out its long tail feathers into a fan, puffs up its body feathers, and struts up and down. It lets its wings droop and shakes them to make a rattling noise. And it gobbles loudly as if to say "Aren't I magnificent?"

Wild turkeys are natives of the Americas. There are just two species. The Ocellated turkey (*Agriocharis ocellata*) is found from the Yucatan Peninsula to Guatemala. It is named for the ocelli, or eye-spots, on its tail. The Common turkey came originally from southern North America and Mexico. It is the ancestor of the domesticated turkey.

A WELL-TRAVELED BIRD

Mexicans were keeping turkeys by the time the Spaniards invaded their country in the 1500s. The invaders took turkeys back to Europe, where they began to be raised widely and became truly domesticated. When Europeans began to settle in North America, they took the domesticated turkeys with them.

The modern breed that developed in Europe from the imported Mexican turkeys is the Bronze. It is named after the color of its plumage, which is grayish-brown and has a metallic sheen. Selective breeding over the years has produced a bird with a broad-breasted, meaty carcass.

Commercially, the most important breed now is the White Holland. This is an all-white bird developed from the Bronze. It originated in England, but is currently intensively farmed throughout the world. It has the same broad, heavy body of the Bronze, but is preferred because it produces a cleaner-looking carcass.

Most other breeds of turkey, such as the Bourbon Red, Narraganset and Norfolk Black, are raised mainly for showing. The world's total turkey population is about 150 million.

TOM, HENS AND POULTS

The male turkey is called a tom or a stag, the female, a hen and a young turkey, a poult. The tom is up to twice the size of the hen.

Most breeds mate naturally, but the White Holland can seldom do so. With its broad breast and short legs, it is not physically able to perform the mating act. Artificial insemination has to be used instead. Turkey eggs are about twice the size of chicken eggs. The poults are hatched well developed and can run about almost at once. When fed on protein-rich feed, they grow very rapidly and reach a weight of as much as 50lb when only a year old.

Both sexes have a bare head and a fleshy wattle at the throat. The knobbly growths on the red head and wattles are called caruncles. Turkeys also have a fleshy growth on the front of the head, often called a dewbill. Toms have a tuft of bristles on the chest and a spur on the legs.

▶A Narraganset, an ornamental breed of turkey bred in the USA. Its plumage is mainly black, but every feather is tipped with white.

▼White Holland Turkeys being intensively farmed in Wisconsin, USA. The males of this breed can achieve weights of up to 33lb when only about 6 months old.

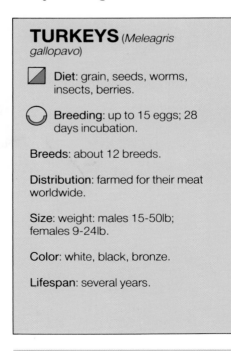

TURKEYS (*Meleagris gallopavo*)

◩ **Diet**: grain, seeds, worms, insects, berries.

◯ **Breeding**: up to 15 eggs; 28 days incubation.

Breeds: about 12 breeds.

Distribution: farmed for their meat worldwide.

Size: weight: males 15-50lb; females 9-24lb.

Color: white, black, bronze.

Lifespan: several years.

DUCKS AND GEESE

It is late at night at an isolated farm. The farmer is sound asleep, unaware of the intruder who is creeping stealthily into the farmyard to rob the farm workshop. Suddenly, a loud honking erupts from closeby. The farmyard geese have heard the intruder and sounded the alarm. With the honking echoing in his ears, the intruder takes to his heels.

Ducks and geese were domesticated around 500 BC. They are now found on farms throughout the world. Both are classed as waterfowl and enjoy swimming. Geese, however, spend more time on the land than ducks and exist quite happily without water.

Ducks and geese are raised mainly for meat, but some are also kept for their eggs. In a number of countries ducks are reared commercially in large numbers, very much like broiler

DUCKS AND GEESE
(*5 main species*)

Diet: plant material, especially seeds, water weed, fish, small animals such as insects and larvae, crustaceans, fish meal, scraps.

Breeding: 6-14 eggs; 4-5 weeks incubation.

Breeds: about 150 breeds and varieties.

Distribution: worldwide in warm and temperate climates.

Size: ducks: weight up to 10lb; geese: up to 30lb.

Color: varies widely; white, black, buff, brown; some vividly multi-colored.

Lifespan: several years.

Species mentioned in text:
Chinese goose (*Anser cygnoides*)
Greylag goose (*A. anser*)
Mallard (*Anas platyrhynchos*)
Mandarin duck (*Aix galericulata*)
Muscovy duck (*Cairina moschata*)

▼Ornamental laying and meat breeds and species of duck Aylesbury (1), from England. Mandarin (2), an ornamental duck from China. Indian Runner (3). Muscovy (4), a native of South America. Pekin (5), originated in China, and a leading commercial breed. Khaki Campbell (6) from Britain, probably the world's best layer. Rouen (7), a French breed raised for meat. Black East India (8), an ornamental duck.

►A gaggle of Toulouse Geese; this breed has particularly short legs. They are large animals that fatten quickly, but they produce only a small number of eggs and these are difficult to hatch.

chickens (see pages 78-81). Geese are raised mainly in small flocks, for they are not really suited to intensive farming methods.

Three out of every four ducks in the world are raised in southern and eastern Asia. They are more suited to the hot, moist climate than chickens and are more resistant to disease.

FINE FEATHERS

Both ducks and geese are densely feathered. They have a thick layer of soft down beneath the outer feathers. For centuries, this down has been used for stuffing mattresses, quilts and pillows. It provides great warmth.

This practice is not as widespread as it was because of the increasing use of man-made fibers. But some flocks are still farmed for their feathers. Often the feathers are plucked off the live birds; this is carried out two or three times a year.

QUACKS AND HISSES

With one exception, all breeds of domestic ducks developed from the common European mallard. The mallard drake (male) is very beautifully colored, with glossy green head and neck, chestnut breast, and a grayish-brown back. The duck (female) is a drab brown, for camouflage.

The modern breed of duck called Rouen has almost identical coloring to the European mallard. But most domesticated breeds look different, although the drakes usually sport the curly tail feathers of the mallard.

The one domesticated duck not derived from the mallard is the Muscovy. Despite its name, this breed came originally from South America. It is not a true duck, and the drake does not have a curly tail. Its most recognizable feature is the rough, bare red region around the head. It can fly a little and often perches on branches.

◄A mixed flock of free-range ducks and geese being fed on grain.

The Muscovy makes quite different noises from other breeds. Normally, female ducks make most of the noise, the typical harsh, rasping "quack." The voice of the drakes is soft and subdued. In the Muscovy the females make little noise, but the drakes hiss loudly. They are much larger than the females and can often be aggressive. Muscovies mate with other breeds, but the offspring, called mule ducks, are usually sterile (are not able to produce offspring).

FOR EGGS, MEAT AND SHOW

Two breeds of duck are outstanding layers. One is the Khaki Campbell, so called because of its tan-brown color. It is an especially lively breed, which often lays more than one egg a day. The Indian Runner is also an excellent layer. It is widely raised in southern Asia. With its relatively long legs, it is suitable for herding, unlike most other breeds.

The white-feathered Pekin is the most important commercial breed raised for meat. It grows rapidly and can reach a weight of over 6lb in less than 8 weeks, and has a mature weight of up to 10lb. The mallard look-alike Rouen, and the Aylesbury, both have a top weight of about 9lb.

Among ornamental breeds is the Call Duck. It is named after the loud call of the female, which was originally used as a decoy by hunters to lure wild duck. This tiny bird, rather like a miniature mallard, can weigh only 14 ounces. The Black East India is another small ornamental domesticated breed. The colorful Mandarin duck is another species, often kept solely for ornament.

GAGGLES OF GEESE

Of all domesticated birds, geese are among the most intelligent. They are very social animals and make good pets. When very young, they will often "imprint" on human beings – they will adopt them as parents. Geese make excellent guard animals. They are constantly alert and have good vision and hearing. A loud honking greets any approaching stranger.

▲A mallard drake and duck stand on the ice of a partly frozen pond. Although ducks are not usually kept as pets, they often frequent waterways and ornamental ponds and lakes throughout northern Europe.

◄A Muscovy duck with a brood of fluffy ducklings. However, the ducklings are common ducks, not Muscovies. The Muscovy is often used as a "foster mother" to incubate ordinary duck eggs.

▼Ducks of the Indian Runner type walking along a track in Bali. They are kept there to weed the rice fields. With their long legs and upright posture, they are more mobile than ordinary ducks.

Two breeds are raised widely for their meat, the Toulouse (originally from France) and the Emden (originally from Germany). The Toulouse has gray plumage, not unlike that of the wild Greylag goose. This goose is the ancestor of most domesticated breeds. The Toulouse is a heavy bird with a mature weight of up to 30lb.

The Emden has white plumage. It is not such a heavy bird, but is a better layer, producing up to 60 eggs a year. The small Chinese goose is an even better layer. It is often crossed with the Emden and other breeds to improve their egg production. The Chinese goose, which can be brown or white, has a long, slim, almost swan-like neck. It is a very lively bird.

NOODLING

In some regions of France young geese are forcibly fed with food, in a process called noodling. Finely ground moist grain is made into large "sausages," or noodles, and forced into the goose's mouth.

This process is repeated several times a day for up to 10 weeks. This makes the goose fatten quickly. It also results in the goose's liver becoming enlarged. From this liver the delicately flavored paste called pâté de foie gras is prepared.

BEES

A week ago the old queen left the hive to swarm and took nearly half the workers with her. Now a new queen is biting its way out of its waxy cell. It eats honey and gains strength. When it sees other new queens emerging, it stings them to death. When it is a week old, it flies from the hive and mates with one or more drones. In the act of mating, the drones die. The queen returns to the hive with enough sperm inside her to fertilize all the eggs she will lay in her lifetime.

Honey gathered from the nests of bees has always been an important food for humans. In Asia, honey is still gathered from the nests of two species of wild bee, the Dwarf honeybee and the Giant honeybee. But most honey now comes from bees kept in hives.

ARTIFICIAL NESTS

The species most kept is the honeybee of Europe and Africa. It was introduced to the Americas and Australias by the early colonists. In the Far East, it is now replacing the native Indian honeybee, which is another species suitable for keeping in hives.

There are about 50 million honeybee colonies kept around the world. Together they produce some 600,000 tons of honey a year. A typical hive, with a population of 50,000 bees, produces 25 to 110lb of honey a year.

Most bees are kept in purpose-built hives that have movable frames to hold the honeycombs. The frames can be removed, and the honey extracted from them, without disturbing the rest of the nest.

Honey is the main product, but other products are also useful. They include beeswax, obtained from the honeycomb; the "royal jelly" fed to queen larvae; and even the venom from the bees' stinging organs.

BEES (4 "domesticated" species)

◼ **Diet:** pollen and nectar from flowering plants.

◗ **Breeding:** honeybees: queen may lay more than 200,000 eggs in a season; workers (undeveloped females) emerge 21 days after eggs laid, drones (males) after 24 days, but queens after only 16 days.

Distribution: worldwide.

Size: length ½-1in.

Color: dark brown, with black bands on abdomen.

Lifespan: worker: about 6 weeks in active season; queen: 1-3 years.

Species mentioned in text:
Dwarf honeybee (*Apis florea*)
Giant honeybee (*A. dorsata*)
Honeybee (*A. mellifera*)
Indian honeybee (*A. cerana*)

▲A "city" of hives on a hillside in Greece. It has been placed there so that the bees can pollinate nearby crops.

►Clothed in complete protective gear, a beekeeper inspects one of the movable frames in the hive.

▼A nest of Dwarf honeybees built on a branch. This common Asian species is not suitable for keeping in hives.

GLOSSARY

Agouti The basic grayish-brown coat color of rats, mice, rabbits and many other wild animals.

Albino An animal whose hair, skin and eyes contain no color pigments. This makes the coat white and the eyes pink.

Ancestor The species from which an animal descended.

Artificial insemination Introducing semen, which contains sperm, into a female animal artificially. It contrasts with natural insemination by normal mating. It is used particularly with cattle.

Bacon Meat from the back and sides of a pig specially prepared by curing.

Bantam A miniature chicken; often a small variety of a standard-sized breed.

Battery hen One of many female chickens (hens) housed in a small cage and reared for egg production.

Beef The flesh of cattle.

Billy The popular name for a male goat.

Bitch A female dog.

Boar A male pig.

Bovine Relating to cattle; comes from the genus name, *Bos*.

Breed To produce offspring; also, to mate selected animals to produce offspring with desired characteristics, such as coat color. Also (noun) a race whose members, when crossed, produce offspring with the same characteristics as the parents.

Breeding The raising and selective mating (crossing) of animals so as to bring about improvements in future generations.

Broiler A young chicken raised by intensive methods for meat.

Brood A term used to describe a hen that is eager to sit on her eggs and incubate them.

Browse To feed on shoots, leaves and bark of shrubs and trees as opposed to grass. *Contrast Graze.*

Buck The male of the rabbit, mouse and some other species of mammal.

Bull The male of cattle.

Bullock A young, usually castrated, bull.

Calf The young of cattle.

Canid A member of the dog family; hence canine, like a dog.

Capon A castrated cock chicken.

Carcass The dead body of an animal.

Carnivore In general, a meat-eater. Specifically a member of the animal order Carnivora.

Carrion Dead and putrefying flesh, often unfit for human food.

Castrate To remove the testicles of a male animal so that it cannot produce offspring. Usually, it loses the urge to attempt to mate.

Cereal Grain crop such as wheat, barley or rice.

Clutch The eggs laid by a bird in one breeding season.

Cob A sturdy, short-legged horse, such as Welsh cob, used for riding and driving.

Cock A male bird.

Crossbreed, or Cross The offspring produced from the mating of two breeds.

Dam The female parent.

Dewlap The loose skin hanging from the throat of some cattle.

Doe A female rabbit, mouse or other species.

Domestication Taming a wild species and gradually altering it by selective breeding to make it more useful to humans.

Dorsal Along the back, for example the dorsal fin of fish.

Draft animal One that draws, or pulls, a wagon or plow.

Drake A male duck.

Ewe A female sheep.

Family the division of animal classification below Order and above Genus.

Fancier A person who keeps or breeds animals as a hobby.

Feral animals Those that have escaped from captivity and returned to live in the wild. Also, descendants of those animals.

Fertilize To introduce sperm to eggs during reproduction.

Fledge Fly for the first time.

Foal A young horse or pony.

Forage crop One grown so that it can be fed to animals, such as hay.

Gander A male goose.

Gelding A horse or pony that has been castrated.

Genus The division of animal classification below Family and above Species.

Gilt A young female pig.

Gosling A young goose.

Graze Feed on grass. *Contrast* Browse.

Habitat The surroundings in which an animal lives.

Hand The measure of height for horses, 1 hand = 4in.

Heat A female mammal is said to come into heat when it is ready to mate and can become pregnant.

Hen A female bird.

Hog The North American term for a pig.

Hybrid The offspring of parents from different breeds.

Incubation The period during which a bird sits on eggs to make them hatch.

Intensive farming A method in which large numbers of animals, such as pigs, cows and chickens, are kept in a limited space and under carefully controlled conditions.

Kid A young goat.

Lamb A young sheep.

Litter A group of animals born at the same time.

Live-bearer A breed of fish (or reptile) that gives birth to live young.

Milt The sperm of a fish.

Mimic An animal, such as a parrot, that imitates the call or sounds of another.

Molt The period when a bird sheds its plumage, or a mammal its coat, and grows a new one.

Mule The offspring of a male donkey and a female horse. Also the offspring of a canary and a finch.

Mutation A change in the genetic material of an animal that brings about a change in its color, form or behavior.

Piebald An animal with a coat of black and white patches.

Plumage The feathers of a bird.

Pony A horse with a height at the withers of 14.2 hands or less.

Pork The flesh of a pig.

Poult The young of fowl, especially turkeys.

Pregnancy The period during which the young grows in the body of a female mammal.

Pup A young dog or Guinea pig.

Ram A male sheep.

Rodent A rat, mouse, or other animal belonging to the animal order Rodentia.

Ruminant A mammal such as the cow that has a stomach with many chambers and containing bacteria which enable it to digest grass. It returns partly digested material to the mouth to be chewed as a cud.

Selective breeding Breeding from selected individuals so as to bring out certain characteristics in an animal,

such as coat color, form or behavior. A pure bred animal is one with genetically similar ancestors. Interbreeding is the mating of genetically unrelated individuals.

Sire The male parent; also, to be the father of offspring.

Skewbald A horse or pony with a coat of brown and white patches.

Sow A female pig after it has borne a litter.

Spawning Mating in fish, in which the male releases its milt (sperm) over the female's eggs.

Species The division of animal classification below *Genus*. Animals of the same species can breed with one another.

Sperm The male sex cells.

Stallion A male horse, not castrated.

Steer A castrated bull.

Tom A male cat or turkey.

Variety A group of animals of the same breed which are usually of similar form and perhaps color.

Withers The highest part of a horse's back, just behind the neck.

INDEX

Scientific names

The first name of each double-barrel Latin name refers to the Genus, the second to the species. Single names not in italic refer to a family or sub-family and are cross referenced to the Common name index.

FURTHER READING

Alderton, D. (1983), *The Cat*, Chartwell, New York.
American Kennel Club Official Publication (1989), *The Complete Dog Book* (21st edn), Howell, New York.
Alexander, R. McNeill (ed) (1986), *The Encyclopedia of Animal Biology*, Facts On File, New York.
Bath, D.L.,Dickinson, F.N., Tucker, H.A. and Appleman, R.D. (1978), *Dairy Cattle*, (2nd edn), Lea and Febiger, Philadelphia.
Berry, R.J. and Hallam, A (eds) (1986), *The Encyclopedia of Animal Evolution*, Facts On File, New York.
Clutton-Brock, J. (1981), *Domesticated Animals from Early Times*, Heinemann, London; University of Texas Press, Austin.
Fogle, B. (1981), *Interrelations between People and Pets*, Charles C. Thomas, Springfield.

Hafez, E.S.E (1975), *The Behaviour of Domestic Animals* (3rd edn.), Balliere Tindall, London: Williams and Wilkins, Baltimore.
Katcher, A.H. and Bec, A.M. (1983), *New Perspectives on our Lives with Companion Animals*, University of Pennsylvania, Philadelphia.
Moore, P.D. (ed) (1986), *The Encyclopedia of Animal Ecology*, Facts On File, New York.
Orme, F.W. (1979), *Fancy Goldfish Culture*, Saiga, Hindhead.
Slater, P.J.B. (ed) (1986), *The Encyclopedia of Animal Behavior*, Facts On File, New York.
Zeuner, F.E. (1963), *A History of Domesticated Animals*, Hutchinson, London, Harper and Row, New York.

ACKNOWLEDGMENTS

Picture credits

Key: *t* top. *b* bottom. *c* center. *l* left. *r* right.
Abbreviations: A Ardea. AN Agence Nature. BCL Bruce Coleman Ltd. HL Hutchison Library. NHPA Natural History Photographic Agency. OSF Oxford Scientific Films. PEP Planet Earth Pictures. RHPL Robert Harding Picture Library.

6*t* HL. 6*b* NHPA. 7*t* Unknown. 7*b* A/J.P. Ferrero. 10 Anthro-Photo. 11 RHPL. 13 A/F. Gohier. 16-17 BCL/K. Taylor & J. Burton. 17 BCL/H. Reinhard. 19*t* BCL/J. Burton. 19*b* Tony Morrison. 20 RHPL. 21 A/M Putland. 22 RHPL. 24, 25 A/J.P. Ferrero. 26*t* A/P.Morris. 26*b* Biofotos/H. Angel. 27 PEP/J. Fawcett. 28 NHPA/S. Dalton. 29 BCL/J. Burton. 30 OSF/R. Jackman. 31 G. Frame. 32 Heather Angel. 33 BCL/J. Burton. 34*t* Tony Morrison. 34*b* BCL/J. Burton. 35 NHPA/E. Janes. 36 BCL/J. Burton. 38 BCL/H. Reinhard. 39 BCL. 40 BCL/A. Compost. 41*t,b* BCL/J. Burton. 42 NHPA/L. Newman. 43 BCL/H. Reinhard. 44 SAL/M. Tibbles. 45 BCL. 47 ZEFA. 48-49 PEP/J. Lythgoe. 50 OSF/G. Thompson. 51, 52 BCL/J. Burton. 53 A. van den Nieuwenhuizen. 54 SAL/M. Kavanagh. 55*t* HL. 55*b* NHPA/E. Janes. 57 HL. 58 HL/S. Porlock. 59 OSF/P.K. Sharpe. 60 HL. 61 B. Hawkes. 62 NHPA/A. Bannister. 63*t* R. Fletcher/Swift Picture Library. 63*b* BCL/E. Dragesco. 65 A/Bomfords. 66-67 A. 68*t* M. Holford. 68*b* BCL. 69*l* BCL. 69*r* G. Bateman. 70*t* HL. 70*b* HL. 73 A/R. Porter. 74 HL. 75*t* OSF/Anna Walsh. 75*b* A/J.P. Ferrero. 76 BCL/M. Viard. 78 A/J.P. Ferrero. 79*t* NHPA/G.I. Bernard. 79*b* A/J.P. Ferrero. 81*t* Zefa/Heilman. 81*b* AN/J.P. Ferrero. 82 BCL/C. Davidson. 83 BCL/N. Tomalin. 85*t* BCL/B. Hamilton. 85*b* OSF/Avril Ramage. 86 Aquila. 87*t* OSF/T. Heathcote. 87*b* RHPL. 88*t* A. 88*b* J.B. Free. 89 OSF/G. Bernard.

Artwork credits.

Key: *t* top. *b* bottom. *c* center. *l* left. *r* right.
Abbreviations: OI Oxford Illustrators Ltd. PB Priscilla Barrett

8-9 K. van den Broecke. 12 PB. 14-15 Peter Warner. 16 OI. 18 PB. 21 PB. 22-23 K. van den Broecke. 28, 31, 37 PB. 39, 42-43 Malcolm Ellis. 46 Johan Lentink. 49, 51 Mick Loates. 56, 58, 59, 64-65, 71, 72, 76-77 PB. 80, 84 Equinox.